D0463045

COLONIAL NEW ENGLAND

HISTORICAL GEOGRAPHY OF NORTH AMERICA SERIES

General Editor
ANDREW H. CLARK
University of Wisconsin

Colonial
New England

A Historical Geography

Douglas R. McManis

Cartographer
Miklos Pinther

New York
Oxford University Press
London 1975 Toronto

Copyright © 1975 by Oxford University Press, Inc.
Library of Congress Catalogue Card Number: 74-21824
Printed in the United States of America

FOREWORD

The steadily expanding fund of scholarly literature of the historical
geography of North America, which is encouraging productive dialogue
between scholars of its sibling disciplines and to which this book makes
a substantial contribution, is proving to be of solid value in a wide
variety of courses in history or geography. The Historical Geography of
North America series, of which this is the fourth volume to appear, is
being written almost entirely by historically-minded cultural and socio-
economic geographers but is aimed as much at historians and their stu-
dents as at geographers. That this has tended to make the writing and
analysis rather more, than less, geographical in emphasis has had the
pleasant bonus that, embryonic as the series yet is, its volumes are finding increasing use as text materials for courses in historical geography
itself. As a result we are introducing into the series a text-study guide
suggesting several course outlines for different approaches to the historical geography of North America and including sample readings, an
annotated bibliography, and a brief introductory essay about the rele-
vance of historical geography to the interpretation of the history and
geography of the United States and Canada.

Professor McManis's study was one of the first envisioned for the
series and we are delighted to see it in print. Its author, a product of
one of our most distinguished departments of geography, at the University of Chicago, is one of the pioneer band of historical geographers
who have responded positively to the challenge presented by the
paucity of materials for the study of colonial geography in the United

States and the difficulty in handling them. Although McManis's first published monograph, *The Initial Evaluation and Utilization of the Illinois Prairies, 1815-1840,* Chicago (1964) was concerned with the trans-Appalachian advance into the Midwest and concentrated on the actions and reactions between settlement and prairie grasslands, he had long been concerned as a scholar with the European descry and discovery along the Atlantic coast from the time of the Vikings through the seventeenth century ("The Traditions of Vinland," *Annals* of the Association of American Geographers (1969) and *European Impressions of the New England Coast, 1497-1620,* Chicago (1972)).

It is obvious that the author knows and loves New England and that, as he has often roamed its highways and byways (if only to move from one archive to another) its geographical evolution, from a relatively lightly occupied land of Indians hunting, fishing, and conducting an extensive, shifting, corn–beans–squash horticulture in pre-Columbian times, to the crowded, industrial ethnic potpourri of today, has been a major object of his imagination and concern. Because New England has meant "Colonial America" to so many Americans for so long, it is perhaps fitting that our first specifically colonial volume should be devoted to that region's development in the seventeenth and eighteenth centuries.

Madison, Wisconsin   Andrew Hill Clark
September 1974

PREFACE

New England is one of the oldest place names for a major American region in use today. It often evokes the stereotyped image of an individualistic sturdy Yankee bounded by Puritanical codes of personal behavior, living primarily in a picturesque rural area distant from and preferable to a crowded urban area. But like most stereotyped images New England's is only partially accurate, for the region has been home to people from many different places who over time have created varied geographic patterns.

Geography, defined as the study of the earth's spatial patterns, has a broad scope. It includes such diverse subjects as man-land relationships and the ecosystems that evolve from—but also determine—the nature of those relationships, the patterns that man has created on the earth and the processes by which he has created them, the description of individual regions or places, the building of theoretical models, and the explanation of spatial phenomena. A field of such diverse investigation must necessarily have many research methodologies. Historical geographers share with geographers who focus on present-day topics the same breadth of subjects and research methodologies, but historical geographers are concerned primarily with past geographic topics, landscapes, or processes. Their concern with the geographic past creates unique problems with which most geographers do not have to cope: although elements of the past may survive into the present in some form, the geographic totality that once existed is gone. Thus historical geographers are confronted with searching out and validating documents appropriate for geographic studies—often a laborious task. Yet a wealth of diverse topics has been successfully presented to the public and much more remains to be investigated.

Although this book bears a regional title, it is not intended to be a traditional regional descriptive geography. It is a study in cultural geography, emphasizing geographic change through time and the processes by which those changes were accomplished. Areal description is necessary to understand the nature of change, but the reader is cautioned to remember that the author conceives of the region as being comparable to the scientist's laboratory, and for this study the actions of man and what one may learn about man as an agent of geographic change are the primary interests. Also this study is based on the assumption that an important task for historical geography is to give depth to interpretation of present-day landscapes by investigating how the dominant patterns developed. Thus the study focuses on a critical formative period in New England's geographical history. It begins with the establishment of European contacts with eastern North America and proceeds to the processes that transformed the indigenous landscape into a distinctive, Europeanized one. Local examples are used to establish the regional geographic patterns and the processes of change; when appropriate the regional patterns of New England are contrasted with those of other major colonial regions, so that the study is not developed in isolation of other colonial seaboard patterns.

Traditional scholarly footnotes have been omitted from the text so that readers can focus more closely on the book's themes. At the end of each chapter a list of suggested readings is provided for those readers who wish to pursue topics in depth. Items in these lists are chiefly secondary writings, each of which contains extensive references or bibliographies to the available primary materials, the ultimate bases on which historical geographies must be constructed.

In writing a book of this sort one is reminded on nearly every page of the many scholars who have studied New England before him, of the many librarians and archivists who aided in research, and the many native New Englanders who insightfully shared their heritage. My mother, Oliva F. McManis, and friends Moya and James Andrews, were pleasant companions during research trips to New England and supplied patient understanding and encouragement during the toils of writing. To Andrew H. Clark, the general editor of this series, I am doubly indebted: first for encouraging me to write this volume and then for his wise and creative criticism of its penultimate draft. To all those persons a heartfelt thanks is expressed.

New York   D. R. M.
November 1974

CONTENTS

LIST OF FIGURES

COLONIAL NEW ENGLAND

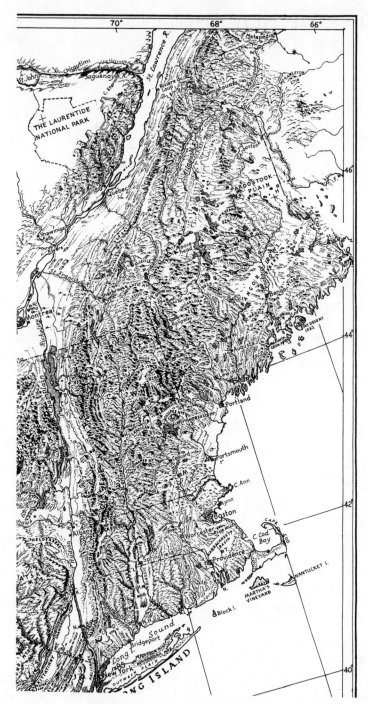

Landforms of New England

1 PRE-SETTLEMENT EUROPEAN CONTACTS

Cultural change of an environment can take place in at least three ways: first, by interaction between (a) ideas, techniques, and tools, and (b) the physical-biotic features of a habitat; second, by diffusion and subsequent adoption of ideas, techniques, and tools from elsewhere; and third, as a result of invasion by alien populations with a distinctly different culture. The transformation of the North American landscape into a predominantly European landscape took place in the third way. The Europeanization of New England was part of a much larger series of similar events taking place throughout most of the Western Hemisphere in the years following the Columbian discovery.

Normally, any large-scale transfer of population from one part of the globe to another is preceded by contacts that establish the existence of the place and provide some knowledge of its physical and cultural characteristics. In New England, settlement followed many decades of such increasing familiarity. The earliest European contacts with the region are only hinted at in medieval European documents or in Indian legends, but on the bases of such evidence some scholars claim that Irish monks visited New England in their search for an earthly paradise. More substantial evidence of pre-Columbian contacts exists for the Norsemen, who during a period in the late eleventh century expanded westward from Norway and Iceland to settle in Greenland. From there, on the evidence of the *Vinland Sagas*, it is generally accepted that they explored portions of the coast of North America. The sagas relate the exploits of the family and friends of Eric the Red and tell of voyages westward of

Greenland, although they are vague about the areas visited and often contradictory about the facts of each voyage. While the principal motive of the Norse voyages to North America was commercial (timber for tree-less Greenland was the principal commodity brought back to the Green-land settlements), at least one of the voyages—that of Karlsefni—was a settlement venture. The motive is given in one of the sagas: "he [Karl-sefni] decided to sail and gathered a company of sixty men and five women. . . . They took livestock of all kinds, for they intended to make a permanent settlement there if possible." The settlement was called Hop, and its location described in another saga as being located "on a slope by the lakeside; some of the houses were close to the lake, and others were further away. They stayed there that winter. There was no snow at all, and all the livestock were able to fend for themselves."[1]

Unfortunately, geographic description within the sagas is so meager and generalized that it is impossible to pinpoint where along the North American coast the Norsemen landed. New England has long been fa-vored as the location of Vinland—the southernmost of the three sections of the North American coast named and described in the sagas—but re-cent archeological investigations have led to interpretations of the sagas that suggest areas in higher latitudes. In any event, that brief flow of Norsemen across the North Atlantic had little or no impact on Euro-peans to the south, from whom the main impetus to explore and settle the Western Hemisphere would come after Columbus. No lasting ex-change between the Old World and the New came from the Norse voy-ages, and by the fifteenth century even the Norse ties to Greenland were lost and forgotten, except as they were told in the tales of heroes.

The first contacts between western Europe and northeastern Anglo-America are equally vague. The voyage of John Cabot and his sons from Bristol, England, into the northwest Atlantic is the earliest post-Columbian voyage on record, although unrecorded visits by fishermen may have preceded the Cabots. But little is known beyond the fact of the voyage itself. A landfall on Newfoundland or Cape Breton Island is disputed, as is the distance the Cabots sailed to the south of their land-fall, although one interpretation of the Cosa Mappemonde (1500), the first European map to show a large land mass north of the West Indies, suggests that they reached a point south of Cape Cod.

1. The first quotation is from the *Greenland Saga;* the second from *Eric's Saga.* See Magnus Magnusson and Herman Palsson (eds.), *The Vinland Sagas: The Norse Dis-covery of America* (Baltimore: Penguin Books, 1965), pp. 65 and 98.

Yet, other than possibly stimulating English interest in the cod fishery, the voyage made little impact on Europeans of the time. Not long after the Cabots sailed, the Portuguese Corte Real brothers might have visited the southeastern coast of New England, but evidence for such a visit is even more fragmentary than the Cabot documents. And like the Cabot voyage, it failed to inspire additional interest in the territory.

The first voyage along the mid-latitude eastern seaboard to produce a record of what was seen was that of Giovanni da Verrazzano in 1524. In the service of Francis I of France, Verrazzano sailed from a point near Cape Fear, the southernmost cape in North Carolina, northward to Cape Breton. He landed at several places and, on returning to France, dispatched a letter to the king recording what he had seen. Two of the landings were in New England—one in Rhode Island at Newport harbor, which Verrazzano called Refugio, the other somewhere along the coast of Maine. At Refugio he and his French crew spent several days revictualing and consorting with the natives, who were friendly and generous, "most beautiful . . . and civilized." These people lived in small villages surrounded by large expanses of cultivated fields; their dwellings were wigwams made of sapling frames covered with reed mats. Less civilized were the natives in Maine, hunters clad in furs who were unfriendly and even hostile toward the crew. But New England, forested only with trees that grew in a cold climate, was a keen disappointment to the French. Although modern researchers are grateful to Verrazzano for his description of the land and the native ways of life, his impressions probably had little impact on his contemporaries; France was too deeply involved in the competition between its sovereign and the Habsburg emperor to be actively interested in the New World. The letter itself seemingly disappeared shortly after it was sent, only to reappear in the nineteenth and twentieth centuries in five variant forms. The fate of Verrazzano's voyage was not too different from the voyages of the Norsemen or the Cabots; it too failed to spark a continuing interest in the regions seen by the explorers. Yet, ideas about the configuration of the eastern coast of North America originating from the voyage survived on the 1529 planisphere drafted by Verrazzano's brother, Girolamo, and on many later maps (see Fig. 1-1).

The voyage of Estévan Gomez, sponsored by Charles I of Spain (usually known as the Holy Roman Emperor Charles V), to find the Northwest Passage suffered a fate comparable to that of Verrazzano's, but for different reasons. Gomez was sent out to explore the mid-latitude coast

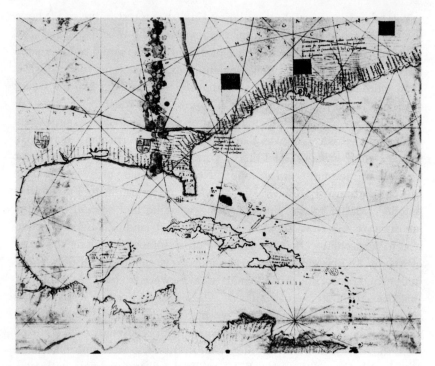

Figure 1-1. Eastern Coast of North America as on the Verrazzano Planisphere of 1529. (*The Vatican Library*)

of North America—then almost totally unkown to the Spanish—in the hopes of finding a viable commercial passage through the American land mass. In 1525 he sailed northward along the coast from Florida. His own log is lost, but other documents indicate that he entered the estuary of the Penobscot River (Maine), which he correctly concluded was not the Northwest Passage. He also noted that the natives practiced a form a transhumance: on a seasonal basis they were alternately hunters-gatherers or fishermen. During the summer they took up residence along the coast to fish, and when winter came they journeyed inland to hunt. On the return voyage from Cape Breton to Spain Gomez carried a cargo of captive Indians,[2] an action that was officially forbidden. Gomez's data were the

2. When Gomez returned to Spain with his captives, or *esclavos* (slaves), as they would have been called in Spanish, someone misunderstood and spread word that the cargo contained cloves (*clavos*). The Royal Court thus thought that he had returned with a shipload of valuable spices. When the truth was learned, Gomez became the target of ridicule and was forced to release the surviving captives.

source of information for the legends on several maps drawn a few years later by Diego Ribero (Cosmographer Royal of Spain and the country's principal cartographer) or his associates. In those legends New England was described as a fertile land capable of growing familiar crops. Yet, because there was no evidence of the Northwest Passage or of treasure, the Spanish chose not to pursue their explorations in the area. Thus the Gomez voyage, like its predecessors, failed to initiate lasting ties between New England and western Europe.

For several decades after the Verrazzano–Gomez voyages the record of European contacts with the New England coast is very fragmentary. Wandering seamen, fishermen, and fur traders were rumored to have touched there, but the surviving records tell little of who they were, what they saw, or where they went. European cartographic treatments of the area reinforce the thesis that little was learned from such contacts. For the most part the area was shown in the style of the Ribero maps, the Verrazzano planisphere, or in a combination of the two styles. These depictions by mid-sixteenth century had become stereotypes and, in the case of Iberian cartography, were perpetuated well into the seventeenth century—long after the configuration of the coast was known and had been accurately drawn in the maps of other national cartographic schools. Despite the failure of the late fifteenth- and early sixteenth-century voyages to establish lasting links between New England and western Europe, they succeeded in convincing at least a few western Europeans that a potentially valuable land mass existed in the mid-latitudes of the New World.

In the last decades of the sixteenth century, New England was known to some Europeans as Norumbega[3] (see Fig. 1-2). A group of Englishmen in the middle years of the reign of Elizabeth I, interested in overseas expansion as a means of promoting new wealth and national prestige, proposed to finance an expedition to be led by Sir Humphry Gilbert to establish an outpost in Norumbega. But before pledging themselves

3. The origin of the word *Norumbega,* and how the word became part of European terminology for a part of North America are still a matter of dispute. Some argue that the word is derived from the Abnaki Indian word *Nolumbeka,* meaning a stretch of quiet water between two rapids. Others claim that it was a remnant of the Norse discovery of North America; still others find its roots in later European origin. Discussions of this problem may be found in W. F. Ganong, "The Origin of the Place-names Acadia and Norumbega," *Transactions* of the Royal Society of Canada, 3rd Series, Vol. XI (1917), Section II, 105–11, and Samuel E. Morison, *The European Discovery of America: The Northern Voyages* (New York: Oxford University Press, 1971), pp. 488–91.

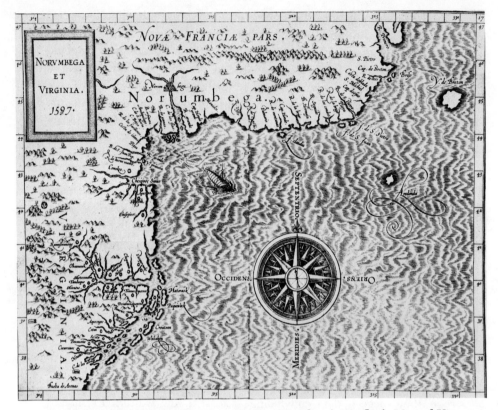

Figure 1-2. New England as Norumbega: Cornelius à Wytfliet's Map of Virginia and Norumbega, 1597. (*The New York Public Library*)

to sponsor the expedition the group attempted to determine the feasibility of the colonial scheme by examining all the data about Norumbega that they could collect. Having no basis to separate fact from fiction, they came up with a description of geographical fact and fancy. Still, the very fact that information was available indicates that contacts during the middle years of the sixteenth century were more numerous than are known to us from surviving documents.

The intertwining of factual and fanciful elements is illustrated by the testimony of David Ingram, one of the few Englishmen of his time to have traveled in Norumbega—or so he claimed. Ingram had been a member of slaver John Hawkins's crew in an ill-fated voyage to the Caribbean in 1567. Shipwrecked somewhere along the Gulf of Mexico, he and two companions alleged that they had walked northeast across the continent to Cape Breton Island, where they were finally rescued. He claimed to have seen fabulous riches—pearls, silver, gold—as well as strange beasts (probably American bison) unknown in England. Ingram's remarks were probably heavily embroidered and were only partially sustained by the reconnaissances of John Walker and Simon Fernandez sent to Norumbega in 1579 and 1580 by the sponsors of the scheme.

The Elizabethan expansionists were motivated by several factors. In addition to the lure of new wealth and hopes of finding the Northwest Passage, they planned to build a naval station from which the Spanish West Indies might be harassed and to establish in Norumbega a settlement modeled on the manorial land-holding patterns of the west Country of England. The scheme never materialized because of Gilbert's pompous and inept leadership: after leaving Newfoundland his fleet turned back without ever reaching Norumbega. Gilbert was lost at sea in 1583 on the return voyage. When his half-brother, Sir Walter Raleigh, revived English interest in planting a North American outpost in the late 1580s, the focus was on latitudes south of New England.

At the close of the sixteenth century two sections of the Atlantic coast were familiar to Europeans: one around Newfoundland and the mouth of the Gulf of St. Lawrence and the other the peninsula of Florida. The mid-latitude region between those two areas was imperfectly known,

A mid-sixteenth century impression of a strange beast in the New World— probably the American bison. (From André Thevet's *Les Singularitéz de la France Antarctique, autrement nommé Amerique.* Antwerp, 1557)

but its geographical characteristics were slowly being revealed by a variety of contacts between it and western Europe. Fishing and the fur trade were the most important of those contacts. The waters around Newfoundland had been fished by men from many ports of northwestern Europe, and some of them had undoubtedly discovered and exploited the banks off New England, but without sharing their knowledge too widely. Similarly, merchants from the ports of Normandy had collected furs from the New England coast, leaving a minimum of documented evidence. Some Europeans continued to believe that the Northwest Passage was to be found there, a belief which persisted into the early seventeenth century. Thus, while Newfoundland was associated in the western European mind with a rich fishery and Florida with an unsuccessful search for a fountain of youth, awareness of the mid-latitude coast of North America was vague, kept alive by a shadowy knowledge of economic potential and legends of vast treasure.

A new era for New England began in the early years of the seventeenth century as the English and the French revived activities along the Atlantic seaboard. Their explorations of the coast and their assessmen:s of its potential represented the first public accumulation of accurate data about its geography and laid the foundations for the later movement of Europeans into New England.

English explorers were first on the scene. In March 1602 the Earl of Southampton sent the *Concord*, a ship commanded by Bartholomew Gosnold to explore and to establish a small post somewhere along the coast of New England, which by that time was known to Englishmen as North Virginia, or the northern part of Virginia. Gosnold sighted the mainland at Cape Neddick in southern Maine (see Fig. 1-3), where a strange sight greeted his English crew: a group of Indians wearing pieces of European clothing paddled out from shore in a Basque fishing vessel. They spoke and understood a few words of English and knew of Placentia Bay, Newfoundland, one of the principal bases of the Newfoundland Banks fishery. Obviously the *Concord's* crew were not the first Europeans to meet those people. Then sailing south, Gosnold anchored near a large sandy headland, where he landed briefly while his men fished and covered the ship's deck with their catch. Because of that bounty the historian of the voyage linked the future of the area to the produce of the sea and foretold a more lucrative fishery than that of Newfoundland. The sandy headland was named Cape Cod by Gosnold, a christening that started the use of European place names in New England.

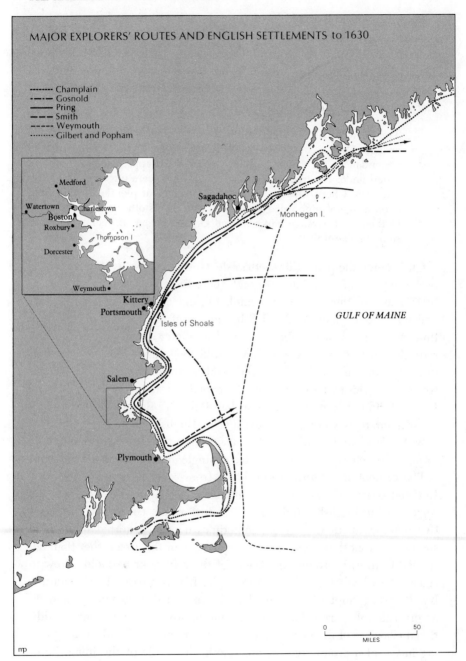

Figure 1-3.

From Cape Cod Gosnold headed south and west toward the islands of
Buzzards Bay. There on a well-wooded island which he considered to be
as fertile as any part of England, Gosnold decided to establish his post.
The island was probably Cuttyhunk, but few today would agree with his
assessment on viewing its barren, windswept landscape. English promoter Brereton described the isle as follows:

> This island is full of high timbered Oakes, their leaves thrise so broad
> as ours; Cedars, straight and tall; Beech, Elme, hollie, Walnut trees in
> aboundance, the fruite as bigge as ours, as appeared by those we
> found under the trees, which had lein all the yeere ungathered; Hasle-
> nut trees, Cherry trees . . . Sassafras trees great plentie all the Island
> over, a tree of high price and profit; also divers other fruit trees, some
> of them with strange barkes, of an Orange colour, in feeling soft and
> smoothe like Velvet. . . .

Christening the place Elizabeth's Isle, Gosnold chose as the site for his
post a tiny island in an interior pond; there the crew traded with the natives, many of them from the mainland, and collected a cargo of furs
and other items such as dried fish and sassafras. Yet when departure
time came, the crew members assigned to winter at the post insisted on
returning to England because they feared the strange land and further,
wished to insure that they received a fair share of the cargo. It is note-
worthy that this first English colonial expedition to arrive safely in New
England did not contain families as had Raleigh's Roanoke colony: commercial interests were then pervasive in English colonial schemes for
New England, and, until the Pilgrims sailed to the New World as family
groups, all such expeditions consisted of single men on economic missions.

The promotional literature resulting from early voyages to the New
England coast had extraordinary influence in shaping the image of the
region in the English mind. That literature rarely contained any negative remarks about the region; sometimes it even distorted mishaps in
such a way that they enhanced the reputation of the area rather than de-
tracted from it. Brereton's treatment of the refusal of Gosnold's crew to
remain on Elizabeth's Isle is an example. It was a case of near-mutiny,
but Brereton emphasized only that the men had returned to share in
a very valuable cargo. Thus he was able to advertise the event as additional evidence of the potential value of the region and add to the growing image of a productive region. Another example of the influence of
promotional literature of the period was the treatment of New England
fisheries. Beginning with Gosnold's voyage and the large amount of cod

taken while the *Concord* was at anchor in Cape Cod Bay, promoters frequently contrasted the fishing potential of New England with that of Newfoundland, concluding that New England's was the greater, both in numbers and quality. Brereton claimed that cod in New England waters were as numerous as in Newfoundland waters and further, that they could be taken in shallower, less dangerous waters. A later promoter using the evidence from the Pring voyage as his authority wrote: "Heere wee found an excellent fishing for Cods, which are better than those of Newfound-land, and withall we saw good and Rockie ground fit to drie them upon." Comparable claims are to be found in later writings by promoters such as Sir Ferdinando Gorges and Captain John Smith.

Encouraged by Gosnold's commercial success, a group of Bristol merchants sent a ship commanded by Captain Martin Pring to the coast in the following year, 1603. Richard Hakluyt the younger, one of the leading advocates of overseas colonization in the late Elizabethan era and the compiler of a monumental work called *The Principall Navigations, Voiages and Discoveries of the English Nation* (1589), wanted the sponsors of the voyage to establish an outpost, but the Bristol merchants were concerned only with immediate profits. Pring left Bristol in March, shortly before Elizabeth I died; thus he was the last seaman to probe the New World who can be called Elizabethan. Landfall was in New England somewhere on the Maine coast among the islands east of Penobscot Bay (see Fig. 1-3); like Gosnold, Pring (as noted previously) also pronounced that the cod fishing in the area was greater than at Newfoundland. He then turned southward, a tack that brought him to the mouths of the Saco, the Kennebunk, the York, and the Piscataqua rivers. Noting that shallow bars blocked the mouths of these rivers and that their courses narrowed rapidly, he was forced to conclude that he had not discovered the entrance to the Northwest Passage. His chief complaint, however, was that he could not find sassafras in the area. The English of the time valued the tree highly, believing that infusions made from its bark and roots had nearly miraculous curative powers, especially for then-exotic maladies such as syphilis, a post-Columbian introduction to Europe. But after entering Massachusetts Bay (inexplicably bypassed by Gosnold), Pring found sassafras in abundance. He anchored in a small inlet, which he called Whitson's Bay, and for seven weeks lingered on, collecting a cargo of bark and roots and testing the area's suitability for English crops by planting small patches of seeds. The seeds sprouted before the ship departed, and, despite his sponsors' disclaimer of any colonial interest, he considered the new plants as evidence of the soil's fertility and the climate's suitability for English habitation. The natives, who practiced some agriculture, were numerous and friendly, and cooperative in helping to amass the cargo. Pring's assessment of the region would prove correct: the inlet in which he tarried was to become the site of the first successful English colony in New England.

After the Pring voyage, the English developed an image of New England as a land of many satisfactory harbors bounded by an ocean teeming with fish from which vast profits could be made. It was thought to be a lucrative source of furs and was rumored to have large expanses of fertile lands where all English crops would flourish. Its forests yielded sassafras and other exploitable timber. Its natives were docile and cooperative, seemingly unable or unwilling to oppose any intruders. That image reached full bloom with Captain George Weymouth's expedition and the promotional literature that came of it.

George Weymouth, like Gosnold, was commissioned by the Earl of Southampton. Although his mission was probably to search for the Northwest Passage westward and southward of the areas visited by Gosnold, he explored only the coast north of Gosnold's landfall. Weymouth left England in the spring of 1605, and sighted land at Nantucket (see Fig. 1-3). But a storm drove his ship northward to Monhegan Island. From there he moved into the St. George's Islands off Penobscot Bay, selected an anchorage on one of the islands, and repeated Pring's experiment with cropping. In the brief time that he and his crew remained there, the plants thrived, and he prophesied that the pine forests of the islands and the mainland would become rich sources of naval stores. Like his predecessors, he also noted the fishing potential. Weymouth also probed the mainland from his insular campsite, navigating for some forty miles a stream he called the "Great River"—probably the St. George's River, but it could have been either the Penobscot or the Kennebec. Proclaiming the "Great River" one of the most magnificent streams in the world, inferior only to the Thames, he also described its tributary lands as among the most fertile and beautiful outside Christendom.

In the aftermath of Weymouth's voyage promotional literature depicting New England as something approximating an earthly paradise reached its apex. Besides glowing reports of the lands he had seen, Weymouth also returned with five kidnapped Indians, who were given to two men interested in sponsoring colonial schemes, Sir John Popham,

Lord Chief Justice of England, and Sir Ferdinando Gorges, governor of Plymouth Fort. The intent was to teach the captives English, returning them with future expeditions to the area as guides and translators.

The English were not alone in their interest in New England during the first decade of the seventeenth century. In 1603 Henry IV of France had granted a fur trade monopoly to Pierre du Gua, Sieur de Monts, for ten years. De Monts and his party put in at Port Royal (Annapolis, Nova Scotia), using it as a temporary base camp from which to survey the shores of the Bay of Fundy, and in the fall of 1604 selected a small island near the mouth of the St. Croix River as the site for their permanent station. They managed to put up a small fort with houses and storage buildings but suffered greatly during the rigorous winter, plagued by scurvy, inadequate provisions, and fire. Samuel de Champlain, who was a member of the party, wisely remarked that an assessment of the country based only on spring and summer conditions omitted a significant feature of the climate—its severe winters. In the spring it was decided to abandon the island site and to seek another in a milder climate.

Ultimately, de Monts wanted a site where a fur post could be maintained on a permanent basis. Such a site required not only local conditions that would permit year-round survival but access to a large fur-producing region with a native population willing to gather and deliver furs to the station. Because the St. Croix island site was thought to be uninhabitable, de Monts and his men made three reconnaissances of coastal New England between 1604 and 1607, sailing as far south as Buzzards Bay on one of the voyages (see Fig. 1-3). Champlain, who accompanied each voyage, kept journals that may be considered the first comprehensive geography of the coast. In 1607 (see Fig. 1-4) he also drew the first accurate map of coastal New England north of Cape Cod, recording the characteristics of the landscape as he saw and perceived them.

As late as the mid-seventeenth century, certain misconceptions about the geography of New England circulated among Europeans. One was the belief that the region was an island, a fancy based on a mid-sixteenth century theory that the Hudson River was a south-flowing branch of the St. Lawrence. The longitudinal spread of the area was too wide, and associated with that misconception was the idea that many New England rivers had their sources in the Lake of the Iroquois (Lake Champlain), which on many maps was placed too far east of the Hudson. Champlain's maps registered the same error, but his explorations along the northern

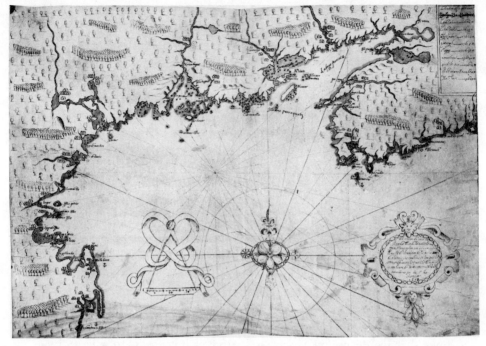

Figure 1-4. Samuel de Champlain's Map of New England and New France, 1607. (*Library of Congress*)

New England coast helped to determine accurately the relationships between it and the drainage area of the St. Lawrence. By observation and information obtained from the natives, he was able to ascertain that streams of northern New England such as the Penobscot and Kennebec rose in the hills and small lakes a short portage distance from the St. Lawrence and did not penetrate far into the interior of the continent. From such information the French rightfully concluded that the rivers of northern New England did not give access to a sizable fur-collection area as did the St. Lawrence, even though the existence of the Great Lakes and the portage routes to the Mississippi drainage was still a matter of rumor. The manner in which the French determined the length of rivers and the size of their drainage basins is also an example of how they, with the aid of the natives, obtained more reliable data than the English, who too often relied solely on their own efforts and perception. During one of the journeys the French learned of the Merrimack River and Massachusetts Bay and its Indian tribes, by requesting a group of southern Maine Indians to draw a map of the territory immediately to the south of theirs. After the first journey native guides were standard attachments to the French exploring parties, as Champlain wrote, "in the hopes of exploring and learning more particularly by their aid what the character of this country was."

At Saco Bay the perceptive French noted a major cultural divide between the natives of New England: south of the area the natives were more numerous and spoke a different dialect than those to the north of it. The southern natives also knew about agriculture and in many cases practiced it, rarely depending on the semi-nomadic hunting-fishing practices of the northern tribes. South of the Merrimack, native villages surrounded by cultivated fields were frequent sights. But the southern Indians were more hostile to the French than the northern tribes had been, and tensions between the two groups culminated in a skirmish near Monomy Point on Cape Cod's southern coast. While that fight did little damage to either side, it was over the long term an important demonstration of the unsuitability of the southern coast for the French purposes. From the standpoint of the French fur traders a large population of any disposition was a negative characteristic in the criteria for site selection. They had observed in the populous, cultivated sections that fur-bearing animals were absent and that the inhabitants displayed little interest in or skills for hunting. There was evidence that the climate of the southern coast was milder than their St. Croix post, but other features of the area precluded its being a long-term source of furs. De Monts's group withdrew from New England, and for a time the French seemed to lose interest in competing for it.

Within a year of Weymouth's return to England the activities of the English along the eastern coast of North America received official sanction: in the spring of 1606 James I issued a royal patent creating two merchant companies to monopolize future English involvement in the area. The first company, assigned the more southerly territory, founded Jamestown (Virginia). The second company, assigned the northern lands, was led by the two men to whom Weymouth had presented the captive Indians, Sir John Popham and Sir Ferdinando Gorges. To verify Weymouth's report they sent two ships on a reconnaissance mission in 1606. Only one of the ships completed the mission and returned with another positive assessment of the northern coast.

Encouraged by this report, Popham and Gorges decided to equip a colonizing expedition the next year. Their plan was typical of the age. A base for collecting export commodities would be established at a coastal

site. Further exploration would be carried out from the base, and inter-
lopers (in this case, the French) would be prevented from sharing the
region's exploitable wealth. Local subsistence was not even considered;
the post would be entirely dependent on supplies sent from England.
Leaders were selected for their social position and status rather than for
their talent. Others in the party were likely to be seamen or adventurers
who could be enticed into a risky scheme by the lure of quick wealth.

The expedition, consisting of two vessels, left England early in August 1607. After a brief stop at Weymouth's abandoned base camp, during which parts of the mainland were explored, the expedition's leaders,
Captain George Popham (cousin of Sir John Popham) and Captain Raleigh Gilbert (son of Sir Humphry Gilbert), chose a site at the mouth of
the Kennebec for their post (see Fig. 1-3). The "Great River" of Weymouth's voyage was not selected, possibly because Weymouth was then
involved in a rival colonial scheme. Neither leader was competent for
the task of developing an economic outpost of empire: Popham was eld-
erly and held Elizabethan fancies about the nearness of China and the
availability of tropical spices, while Gilbert was his father's son in per-
sonality and ability.

A small fort with shelters and storehouses was built, but the men soon
divided into quarreling groups, refusing to cooperate in the tasks of survival or to perform the duties for which they had been sent. Gilbert did
explore some more of the mainland, but his reports added nothing new
to the catalogue of the region's resources. Fertile lands, abundant fish,
and a vast forest which others before him had praised were all he could
report. The Popham colonists (the colony is identified either by the
name of its principal sponsor or by the name Sagadahoc, which the estuary of the Kennebec was then called) probably lacked the fortitude
and resolution needed to see the post survive and flourish. And in the
spring the men found themselves without leaders: George Popham had
perished during the winter and Raleigh Gilbert had decided to return to
England to claim an inheritance. Sir John Popham had also died that
spring, and with his death the political and financial status of the company became uncertain. So it is not surprising that the men who had
lasted out the winter decided to abandon the colony and return to England. At Jamestown the settlers had made a comparable decision, but at
Sagadahoc there was no sudden arrival of relief to dissuade the men
from their decision. Thus the second English post to be established in
New England was abandoned within a year of its founding.

Sagadahoc had failed for many reasons—inadequate preparation, divided and ineffectual leadership, no exports to satisfy sponsors and investors. But word was rapidly spread throughout England that the men left because of the harsh winter, that Englishmen could not survive a rigorous winter, and that the area was uninhabitable except in the summer. The currency given those thoughts destroyed the growing reputation of New England as a land suitable for English colonization. Even the propagandists who had produced the favorable image were unable to prevent its dissolution in the aftermath of the colony's failure.

New England, however, was not completely abandoned by the English. Ships continued to visit its coast to collect furs and fish; Sir Francis Popham, heir of Sir John, repeatedly sent his ships to trade there. Adventurers such as Henry Hudson still sought the Northwest Passage in those latitudes, and Virginians came annually for fish to supplement their colony's food supply. On one such voyage in 1613, Sir Samuel Argall came upon a group of Frenchmen, including two Jesuit priests, who had been sent out to start a mission on Mount Desert Island. He attacked and captured the entire party.[4] Later he returned to burn Port Royal, Nova Scotia. His actions, which were to enforce England's territorial claims against French encroachments, marked the opening of the imperial conflict between the English and the French for dominance in northeastern North America, a conflict which continued intermittently until 1763.

Shortly after Argall's enforcement of English claims, Captain John Smith entered the history of New England. Seemingly in disgrace for his conduct in the management of Virginia or at least feeling himself inadequately repaid for saving the Virginia colony, Smith, always a controversial figure, sought a new career. He found it as the publicist for New England settlement. Although he spent only three months exploring the coast of New England, he devoted the last fifteen years of his life to promoting the area, motivated by the unfulfilled hope that he would be sent to New England as the leader of a new colony.

In the summer of 1614 an English merchant wishing to break the traditional fish merchants' monopoly in England dispatched Smith to New England to take whales. But Smith disregarded orders, instead exploring

4. Argall found the French squabbling among themselves about the best way to start the mission. One group was arguing that a fort should be erected first, while another wanted to start crop cultivation before any buildings were erected. Evidently the French were so busy with their internal quarreling that they failed to notice the approach of the Virginians.

Figure 1-5. Captain John Smith's Map of New England, 1614. (*The Beinecke Rare Book and Manuscript Library, Yale University*)

the coast from Penobscot Bay to the northern part of Cape Cod (see Fig. 1-3). Since most of that area had already been visited by English voyagers, Smith made no new discoveries in the region; his role was to be that of the first Englishman to survey the coast as a unit and to evaluate it in terms which differed from those of his predecessors, judgments which have stood the test of time. As a propagandist he publicized his opinions in his writings and on his famous map of New England (1616) (see Fig. 1-5). His countrymen knew the area as the northern part of Virginia or North Virginia; Smith was the first to call the area New England.

John Smith's assessment of northern New England was more realistic than previous English ones, in part because he had as perspective for his judgments greater knowledge of North America. He repeated the prophecy of lucrative fish and forest resources and noted that other parts of the world at the same latitudes were fertile and productive—a frequent argument traceable to the classical division of the world into latitudinal zones. But, in contrast to earlier promoters, he did not boast that the area's potential was equal to or only equaled by the best parts of England. He sensibly reserved his most laudatory remarks for southern New England.

Smith labeled the coast of Massachusetts Bay "the Paradise of all those parts," basing his claim on the evidence of a large population residing there, good harbors, and cultivated fields. He noted that only the lack of an industrious people (in other words, the English) prevented the area from realizing its full potential. What better place to recommend for a colony than an area already supporting large numbers of people in an agricultural economy? That dream of a new England was illustrated on his map by the numerous settlements with English place names. At the same time, Smith was aware that a colony needed investors and that investors wanted profits. Although he correctly pointed out that the fur trade would never prosper in the south, he envisioned a profit from fishing that would surpass Newfoundland's, a not very original idea borrowed from pre-Popham Colony promoters. In his dream of a southern New England developed by resident Englishmen he predicted the events of Europeanization, the cultural changes wrought by English migration. Smith lived to see the changes begin, but he had contributed only words to convince a dubious public that it was possible.

While Smith was systematizing English knowledge of the eastern coast of New England, Dutch explorers were active along its southern coast. Their presence helped the English to realize how tentative were their claims without occupation. In 1614 Adrian Block (after whom Block Island was named) sailed into Long Island Sound from the west and determined for the first time the configuration of the southern coast. Dutch explorers also found the Connecticut River, which they recognized as the largest stream to enter the Sound, and called it Fresh River. With the English they shared the task of exploring Narragansett Bay, but like the English failed for several years to grasp completely the intricate land-water nature of the coast from that bay to the eastern side of Cape Cod.

Other Englishmen besides Smith shared renewed enthusiasm for New England in the second decade of the seventeenth century. Time had dispelled much of the unfavorable image produced by the collapse of the Popham colony. Sir Ferdinando Gorges, after seven years of half-hearted patronage of the Virginia Company, turned his attention once again to New England and remained one of its steadfast defenders until his death during the English Civil War. But he wisely had shifted the focus of his activities south of Casco Bay in Maine; perhaps he too had lingering doubts about the habitability of the northern coast or did not want new schemes to be burdened with old prejudices. Like Popham's heir and others, he sent expeditions after furs and fish which served to remind England of the commercial gains to be made from New England and, in the hope of proving the area south of Casco Bay habitable, he had his agent Richard Vines winter at Saco Bay in 1616–17. The hardy Vines survived in good condition, but his example failed to dislodge doubts about the area's habitability. Despite evidence of commercial profit provided by fishermen who had established temporary camps on off-shore islands such as Monhegan and the Isles of Shoals, Gorges by 1620 had still not been able to start a colony. He had been able, however, to muster enough support to restore the moribund second (Plymouth) company and to obtain a new patent, which chartered the Council for New England. The Council was presided over by a powerful Puritan, the Earl of Warwick.

One important result of European contacts during that decade was the spread of disease among the coastal natives. Sometime in 1616 or 1617 a mysterious plague, possibly measles or scarlet fever, spread among the Indians from Cape Cod northward; the inland natives seemed to have been spared. Particularly in the southern section, where the first permanent English settlers would arrive, the native coastal population was decimated. Some tribes were totally wiped out. As in many epidemics, it was most destructive where the population was most numerous and densely settled. By 1620 the thriving, populous agricultural villages that Champlain and Smith had seen were empty and deserted. Only a few pitiful survivors of the plague inhabited the southern New England coast when English settlement began.

Suggested References

Arber, E. (ed.). *Travels and Works of Captain John Smith*, 2 vols. (Edinburgh: John Grant, 1910).

Barbour, Philip L. *The Three Worlds of Captain John Smith* (London: Macmillan, 1964).

Hakluyt, Richard. *The Principall Navigations Voiages and Discoveries of the English Nation*, 2 vols. (Cambridge: Cambridge University Press, 1965, facsimile reprint of 1589 edition).

Levermore, Charles H. (ed.). *Forerunners and Competitors of the Pilgrims and Puritans*, 2 vols. (Brooklyn, N.Y.: New England Society of Brooklyn, 1912).

McManis, Douglas R. *European Impressions of the New England Coast 1497–1620* (Chicago: University of Chicago Department of Geography Research Series, 1972).

———. "The Traditions of Vinland" (*Annals* of the Association of American Geographers, LIX (December, 1969), 797–814).

Morison, Samuel E. *The European Discovery of America: The Northern Voyages* (New York: Oxford University Press, 1971).

———. *Samuel de Champlain: Father of New France* (Boston: Little, Brown, 1972).

Preston, R. A. *Gorges of Plymouth Fort* (Toronto: University of Toronto Press, 1953).

Quinn, David B. *England and the Discovery of America 1481–1620* (New York: Alfred A. Knopf, 1974).

Sauer, Carl O. *Sixteenth Century North America* (Berkeley, Calif.: University of California Press, 1971).

Thayer, Henry O. (ed.). *The Sagadohoc Colony* (Portland, Maine: Gorges Society, 1892).

Williamson, J. A. (ed.). *The Cabot Voyages and Bristol Discovery Under Henry VII* (Cambridge: Cambridge University Press for the Hakluyt Society, 1962).

Wroth, Lawrence C. *The Voyages of Giovanni da Verrazzano 1524–1528* (New Haven, Conn.: Yale University Press, 1970).

2 BEGINNINGS OF ENGLISH SETTLEMENT

The standard diffusion model provides a theoretical framework in which the first phase of the Europeanization of New England may be examined. From a place of origin a group of people migrate to a new location where a point of contact is made, and, perhaps, a new cultural hearth is established. From that point of contact further diffusion may occur, but each successive movement usually has less volume than the original movement as the founding group splinters. The spatial aspects of the model relevant to the diffusion of Europeans and their ways of life throughout New England include place of origin, pattern of movement, site of introduction and, at a later time, splintered dispersal throughout the hinterland from that point. The diffusion model is equally applicable to other major colonial regions or individual colonies along the Atlantic seaboard, although the details of each pattern may vary from those of New England. For example, in comparison with the Middle Colonies, colonial New England lacked ethnic variety; on the other hand it was similar to the Delaware Valley in that later migrations to the area were more influential than the early ones. It was also similar to the Southern Colonies in that the initial point of contact proved less satisfactory than settlements founded at a later time, but was significantly different from them in the composition and social and economic characteristics of its migrants.

On the eve of permanent English settlement in New England, many groups of Englishmen were interested in the area. Yet few of them thought of the New World as a permanent home for their countrymen.

Interest focused on more tangible and profitable things. Nationalists saw overseas expansion and colonies as necessary symbols of English power and prestige. To adventurers and speculators the new land was a possible stage for their activities. Traditional economic groups saw the possibility of augmenting England's critical raw materials; others saw an opportunity to challenge the traditional sources and controls of English manufactures and commerce through investment and exploitation. English regional interests, fearful and jealous of commercial dominance by Londoners, competed for a share of the profits from overseas expansion. Although the Crown was not directly involved in the expansion, it exercised its authority and desires through conditions stipulated in letters-patent chartering mercantile companies to carry out colonial schemes. Those conditions included the vague and sometimes contradictory areal limits within which a company could be active, the amount of authority a company might exercise in its territory, and the designation of individuals or group responsible for directing the company. Such motives and policies had inspired several English groups to sponsor exploration of the New England coast before 1620, as has been observed in Chapter I. Men such as Gosnold, Pring, Weymouth, and Smith were but agents of the sponsoring groups. And the actions of those men in regard to New England reflected but one aspect of the political, social, and economic forces that were reshaping Stuart England.

Religious dissension had little place in motivating English colonization before 1620. Ironically, it was the primary force in the beginnings of permanent settlement in New England, and the theocratic nature of New England's development was one of the hallmarks of New England's distinction as a unique seaboard colonial region. Not since the middle years of the reign of Elizabeth I, when Sir George Peckham proposed Norumbega as a refuge for English Catholics, had anyone seriously thought of the New World as a haven for English religious unorthodoxy. The idea of the English way of life being transported abroad was strange enough in the early seventeenth century, but when it was combined with the idea of providing a haven for religious dissenters, the result was a concept almost without precedent in English thought, a concept foreign to the prevailing ideas of how a colony should function and who should occupy it.

Religion became a major force in New England's destiny more by accident than by intent. The Pilgrim migration of 1620 differed radically from any previous English migration to the New World. The Pilgrims were a group of Englishmen who banded together to exile themselves to North America. The entire fabric of their being was to be transported— and, if fate were kind, to be transported to a location where they could remain English yet practice a religious creed disavowed at home. They scheduled or projected no return. The land to which they sailed was henceforth to be their home. No matter how ill-prepared they were—few of the Pilgrims had had any immediate experience with agriculture— their primary goal was to sustain themselves, not to exploit the land for commerce. If things had gone as planned, their colony would have been located somewhere within the limits of the Virginia Company territory, but the era's imprecise sailing techniques brought the Pilgrims to the shores of New England.

The Pilgrims were English Separatists who had migrated first to Holland in search of a place where they could practice their creed without governmental interference. But after a decade or more in Holland, they chose to resettle in English territory because they were concerned about the potential loss of their English identity. Unlike the Puritans, who wanted to reform the Church of England by removing royal and episcopal controls and by abolishing rituals and dogmas which they considered Roman Catholic, the Pilgrims had broken completely from the Church of England. Yet they did not dispute the sovereignty of the Crown nor did they disavow loyalty to it. They simply wanted the liberty to worship as they pleased. The Crown ultimately refused them liberty of conscience but promised not to molest them in their distant exile.

After three years of futile attempts to transfer themselves to Virginia, the Pilgrims became associated with Thomas Weston, a wealthy ironmonger who headed a group of Londoners wanting to establish a plantation in Virginia. The Weston group offered to handle the financial and business side of the venture; in return the Pilgrims were to ship furs and fish to England until their debts to Weston were repaid. Because the Pilgrims were for the most part poor folk without money, credit, or connections to pay for the journey to North America, Weston's offer was accepted, a move that indebted the colonists for years to come. Weston's patent was from the Virginia Company, and, although it did not specify where the Pilgrims were to locate, they must have planned to settle south of 41° N—in other words, south of New England. Many authorities, however, dispute this interpretation of the Pilgrims' original intent.

Early November 1620 found the Pilgrims aboard the *Mayflower* off Cape Cod, which by then was well enough known to the English navigators to be recognized by members of the crew. After a vain and nearly disastrous attempt to sail south through the dangerous, shoally waters on the eastern side of the Cape, the *Mayflower* put into Provincetown harbor, where it lay at anchor for a month. The decision to remain there and to seek a suitable place to settle began the series of decisions that finally resulted in the establishment of Plymouth as a cultural hearth. Time, of course, would prove this first permanent settlement in New England to be less influential than later ones.

The Pilgrims appeared to have been completely ignorant of the geographic characteristics of the area in which they found themselves. After the initial landing at Provincetown, three exploring expeditions were sent ashore to assess the environs and to find a satisfactory site for the colony. The Pilgrims did not know that the coastal tribes had been almost completely decimated only three to four years before their arrival. As the newcomers roamed the Cape, they frequently encountered evidence of recent human occupance—fields with plant stubble, wigwams, caches, burial sites, European goods—all deserted, abandoned, unused. While they were fearful of attacks from the natives, they were also amazed and perplexed that they did not see them, except for a few fleeting forms at a distance. Among other things, the Pilgrims wanted to interview the natives to get more information about the area. Once an exploring party was attacked, but its members defended themselves without loss. So the task of exploring proceeded without the benefit of native advice. In selecting the colony's site, the Pilgrims put a high premium on the location of abandoned Indian fields and other evidence of indigenous land use as guides in the critical decisions that led to the selection of the colony's site.

Other features of the depopulated landscape that the Pilgrims noted were flora, fauna, and drainage patterns. Many plants and trees were known to them in Europe. Animal life also seemed familiar, although they were probably disappointed that fur-bearing animals were not more in evidence. As one scholar has remarked, nowhere could the English have gone so far across an ocean and found by chance a region containing so many natural features recognizable from their European heritage. Such a situation did much to reduce the impact of strangeness and allowed them to continue almost uninterrupted many traditional practices.

In the promotional literature resulting from earlier English voyages to the coast the geographic emphasis had been on exploitable commodities and occasionally on the aesthetic quality of the landscape. The Pilgrims were the first group of Englishmen to assess a portion of New England solely from the viewpoint of how well it might sustain their way of life. Their concerns were with the utilitarian features of the landscape. Availability of water was a prime criterion in their judgment of possible colonial sites. Ignorant of the region's long-term climatic pattern and of the characteristics of seasonal precipitation, they sought to base their water supply on as many surface sources as possible. Wells were tedious to dig and could dry up. Springs, streams, and ponds in some combination were needed close to the settlement site. Other criteria for the site were a sheltered harbor deep enough for the shallow-draft ocean vessels of the time, fertile soils, accessible timber, and enough open area around the buildings to insure against surprise attacks.

One axiom of cultural geography is that group decisions about settlement sites, land use, and physical structures represent a critical stage in landscape evolution, a stage that occurs before any changes are made in the landscape. The Pilgrims left a classic example of group behavior at that stage, when, after the second exploring survey, they met as a group to decide what to do. It must be remembered that they faced unusual problems because of the lateness of their arrival—winter had already begun and food supplies on the Mayflower were short. They needed shelter for the winter, and the colony had to be in form by spring so that cropping could start. Still, they were reluctant to decide hastily, knowing they would have to move to another site if the first choice proved unsatisfactory. Besides, they might find a better site later on. A passage from *Mourt's Relation* summarizing the Pilgrims' debate illustrates succinctly the variables they considered in reaching a decision:

> Having thus discovered this place, it was controversall amongst us, what to doe touching our . . . setling there; some thought it best for many reasons to abide there. As first, that there was a convenient Harbour for Boates, though not for ships. Secondly, Good Corne gound readie to our hands, as we saw by experience in the goodly corne it yeelded. . . . Thirdly, Cape Cod was like to be a place of good fishing, for we saw daily great Whales of the best kind for oyle and bone, come close aboord our Ship. . . . Fourthly, the place was likely to be healthfull, secure, and defensible. But the last and expeciall reason was, that now the heart of Winter and unseasonable weather was come upon us. . . .
>
> Others againe urged greatly the going to *Anguum* or *Angoum*,[*] a place twentie leagues off to the Northwards, which they had heard to

---

[*] Probably somewhere on the north shore of Massachusetts Bay.

be an excellent harbour for ships; better ground and better fishing. Secondly, for any thing we knew, there might be hard by us a farre better seate, and it should be a great hindrance to seate where we should remoue againe. Thirdly, the water was but in pondes, and it was thought there would be none in Summer, or very little. Fourthly the water there must be fetched up a steepe hill; but to omit many reasons and replies used heere abouts; It was in the ende concluded, to make some discovery within the Bay. . . .

While on the third expedition the survey party sought refuge from a storm in a small bay on the western side of Cape Cod Bay. Unknowingly they had entered Whitson's Bay (named Plymouth Bay on the Smith map of 1616), where Pring had camped more than a decade earlier. They stayed the night on the first land found inside the sand bars, which the next day they recognized as an island—now called Clark's Island. After exploring the area around the bay, they returned to Provincetown to persuade the others that a site along the bay would be the best place to locate their settlement. Of three possible sites on the shore of the bay, the present site of Plymouth was chosen as having the most suitable combination of characteristics for the new colony. The sheltered bay provided the necessary harbor, although it later proved too shallow for large ocean-going vessels, a fact which was to reduce Plymouth's trade.[1] Stretching inland were considerable expanses of cleared land thought to be fertile because of evidence of recent Indian cultivation. Uncut forest was close enough to provide lumber for buildings, fences, and fuel yet distant enough so that it could not serve as cover for surprise attacks on the village. A hill near the shore was high enough to command a view beyond the bay so that foreign attack from the sea could be detected. A spring, a stream, and a nearby pond guaranteed the water supply. On December 6, 1620, the *Mayflower* entered Plymouth Bay and the colonists disembarked to begin the task of establishing themselves in their new homeland.

1. Plymouth's failure to become a major trading center is related to more factors than the inadequacies of its harbor. Although the colony was initially successful in the fur trade (the proceeds of which were used to pay off the debt to the Weston group), the Plymouth colonists did not broaden the base of that trade as it waned. Instead, when the arrival of the Puritans offered the Pilgrims a market for their agricultural surplus, they chose that option. Meanwhile, trade quickly became a major activity in the Massachusetts Bay Colony, where capital, qualified merchants, and connections with potential markets existed. Such human and economic resources were lacking among the Plymouth settlers; thus, even if some of them had wanted to challenge the hegemony of Boston in trade, the absence of needed resources precluded Plymouth's becoming anything but a minor local trading center.

They built a small, compact village with houses of sawed timbers facing a single pathway. The thatched roofs of the buildings were to be the cause of many fires. Later a palisade was erected on the hilltop. A meetinghouse that served for both civil and religious functions was the only other public building. In the spring an Indian wandered into their midst. He spoke a few words of English and informed them that he was the sole survivor of the Paxtet tribe upon whose lands the Pilgrims had settled. He showed them the Indian methods of planting maize—hilling with sticks and placing fish in the hills for fertilizer. The settlers continued to use Indian cropping methods until they were able to prepare the fields for English methods of agriculture; they were but the first of many emigrants to adopt temporarily Indian agricultural methods in a frontier situation. Originally the Pilgrims numbered a hundred persons, but more than half of them died during the first winter. The survivors persisted in their decision, and natural increase and immigration slowly increased the population.

Once established, the Pilgrims turned to other tasks, particularly their responsibilities to the Weston group. Fishing was never to be profitable for them; they lacked the skills and equipment to rival fishermen on the northern coast, and marketable fish in local fresh waters were in short supply. They were markedly successful, however, in the fur trade. Making friendly contacts with local Indians through the Wampanoags and their chief, Massasoit, Plymouth colonists led by Edward Winslow made trading expeditions, first into Massachusetts Bay and later into Narrangansett Bay, to collect furs. In 1627 the first Plymouth trading post was established at Aptuxet on the southwest coast of Cape Cod, where it commanded a portage route across the Cape. The Plymouth ventures into the Narrangansett region brought the Pilgrims into competition with the Dutch, who were already trading there. Isaac De Rasieres, an official at New Amsterdam, visited Plymouth in 1627 in an effort to divert the English from the region, but apparently all he accomplished was to teach the Plymouth colonists to use wampum in their exchanges with the Indians, an action that enhanced rather than reduced their competition. In 1629 Plymouth opened a second post on the Kennebec River near present-day Augusta, Maine, on a tract confirmed to the colony by its new patent from the Council for New England. The high point of Plymouth's fur-collecting activities was the establishment of a third post on the Connecticut River in 1633 at the site of Windsor. Again, their action was a direct challenge to the Dutch, who not only claimed rights to the area by discovery but who also operated a trading post on the opposite bank (present-day Hartford) on land purchased from the Pequot tribe. The knowledge of southeastern New England that Winslow and others acquired from the fur trade was instrumental in providing the fairly precise definition of Plymouth's western boundary as stated in the 1629 patent from the Council for New England. In general the rapidity with which the Pilgrims had to expand their fur trading activities beyond the boundaries of the colony was proof to all future colonists and exploiters that Smith's assessment of the southern portion of New England as inadequate for fur trade was correct.

For a decade the Plymouth colony remained the major focus of settlement in New England. It would always be the cultural hearth of New England, but once the Pilgrims had demonstrated that permanent settlement was possible, the mainstream of events quickly bypassed the colony. In later years the Pilgrims and their descendants were but subsistence farmers, only minimally involved in the economic changes that produced a wide range between wealth and subsistence among their neighbors. Yet, if they had failed, others might not have come to New England so readily.

The Pilgrims' self-imposed isolation and loneliness did not last long. In 1622 Weston sent another group, primarily men, to Plymouth, but they soon removed to Wessagussett, now Weymouth, in order to develop a fishing and fur-trading center. The venture did not survive the winter. At about the same time a Captain Wollaston with men and servants established himself at Passonagessit (Quincy), but he soon left for Virginia. His campsite, called Mount Wollaston, was then taken over by Thomas Morton with his band of fur-traders and the name changed to Merry Mount. Tales of licentious behavior, including dances around a Maypole, found their way to the Pilgrims, and a small troop led by Miles Standish was dispatched to put an end to Merry Mount—because of its bad moral character, if one accepts the Pilgrim version. Not to be overlooked was Morton's great popularity with the Indians, who preferred to do business with him. By ousting Morton the Pilgrims not only protected the morals of New England, they also got rid of a successful rival in the fur trade. These attempted settlements differed from Plymouth colony in that they were exclusively economic outposts and lacked religious cohesion. Like the earlier Popham colony, they floundered (with the exception of the Morton enterprise) because of inadequate provisions, internal dissensions, and improper staffing.

In 1623 the Council for New England, under the auspices of Sir Ferdinando Gorges, also attempted to establish a settlement. In the fall of that year a party led by Robert Gorges, son of Sir Ferdinando, arrived in New England. The younger Gorges had been appointed Governor-General of New England and had been granted a large tract of land on the north shore of Massachusetts Bay. But instead of settling there, he and his party wintered at the abandoned camp of the Weston group at Wessagussett, where there existed some rudimentary shelter. The Gorges group was more representative of English society than were the Pilgrims, for it contained gentlemen, mechanics, farmers, traders, and clergymen. Gorges himself was a professional soldier; rank and birth, not talent, had earned him the leadership. Landing in September, the colonists suffered through a miserable winter. In the spring Gorges, who had proved himself incapable of leadership, returned to England, leaving the rest to drift in small groups to fishing stations on the northern coast of New England. The first effort of the Council for New England to colonize its lands had failed, and one can but speculate how different the history of New England might have been if the shores of Massachusetts Bay had been occupied by non-Puritans before 1630.

The Council for New England was primarily the creation of the elder Gorges, who had first entered the history of New England as a member of the second Virginia Company. When by 1620 he found that moribund company inadequate for his purposes, he petitioned the Crown for a new charter. As member of the landed class, his schemes for New England stressed land ownership and income from it rather than trade, agriculture, or fishing. He ultimately desired to transplant the manorial system of which he was a part into the New World. But in his long, failure-filled career, he never realized that his archaic ideas would never take hold in New England. Opposition within the English government delayed the granting of the new charter until 1621. The original Council had forty members, none of them merchants. Only later, when funds were needed, were mercantile interests allowed to purchase their way into membership.

By the charter of 1621 the Council for New England was granted all the territory between the fortieth and forty-eighth parallels of north latitude to the Western Ocean. As often happened in the early seventeenth century, these bounds overlapped previous Crown grants in the New World. Within that huge territory the Council owned all unallotted lands and held powers of local government. When it returned its charter to the

Crown in 1635, however, land grants, not governance or settlement, were the principal legacies of its activities. Most of the grants had been made to the powerful lords and gentry on the Council and were never taken up. Some bounds of the grants overlapped one another and were the source of later legal conflicts among settlers and colonies. But a few of the grants were used, and these had considerable impact on later developments, particularly in Maine and New Hampshire.

While the elder Gorges sought support for his schemes and the Council for New England pretended that it was an effective real estate agent, independent settlements began to appear in the Council's domain. Plymouth was one such example, although technically it was started before the Council's patent was approved, gaining legal status when Plymouth leaders, with the aid of the Earl of Warwick, obtained a charter from the Council in 1629. Known as the "Old Charter," it remained the basis of Plymouth's legal existence until the colony was absorbed into Massachusetts Bay province in 1691.

Other examples were small fishing stations located north of Cape Ann in the many sheltering coves of the islands and mainland. Consisting of clusterings of fishermen's shacks, salt works, and storage facilities, the stations had only a few year-round residents. Most of the fishermen plying the route between the fishing banks and Europe called in only periodically. The most important island stations were on Monhegan and the Isles of Shoals; these and other offshore settlements flourished until the 1640s, after which time the mainland settlements became more important.[2]

Among the few significant and lasting actions of the Council was the joint grant to the elder Gorges and John Mason on 1622 of all the land between the Merrimack and Kennebec rivers. The grant introduced into the history of New England Captain John Mason, who unlike Gorges had some direct notion of the area's geography because he had previously served as Governor of Newfoundland. The huge tract was divided

2. Several factors accounted for this shift in focus: (1) As settlements expanded northward along the mainland they offered the colonists a broader base of economic activities than did the offshore islands. Agriculture, for example, could be practiced more widely, and employment in timber operations or shipbuilding was also available. (2) Direct sailings between the islands and fishing ports of western Europe declined as aggressive merchants of the Bay Colony appropriated a large share of the fishing activity and funneled it to the mainland ports. (3) The fisheries themselves were expanding, and the offshore islands were unable to accommodate that expansion; thus newcomers to the fisheries had little choice but to establish their ports and drying stations on the mainland.

between them in 1629, an act that resulted in the political separation of
New Hampshire and Maine. Mason received the land south of the Piscataqua River, while Gorges retained the land to the north. The conflicting and territorially overlapping nature of many of the Council's
grants was well illustrated by two grants made in 1623 in the same area
—one of them to David Thompson and a group of merchants in Plymouth, England, the other to the Laconia Company for trade throughout
the Council's domain. Thompson settled at the mouth of the Piscataqua,
but he later found an island in Boston harbor more to his liking and,
leaving his fellow colonists at the Piscataqua settlement, took his family
to Thompson Island, where his widow greeted the Puritans on their arrival. The rest of Thompson's group was absorbed into Mason's claim.
The Laconia Company established its colony at Dover Point, where the
Piscataqua River and a large inlet known as Great Bay merge. The Company never fulfilled its promise to trade in the interior, and its settlement
—like the others along the lower Piscataqua—was principally active in
fishing and fish-curing. Eventually the conflicting legalities of the Council's overlapping grants were resolved when the settlements along the
southern banks of the Piscataqua were united into the nucleus of the
province of New Hampshire.

The Council's grant of fishing rights and territory for a station at Cape
Ann was crucial to New England's future. In 1623 a group of men from
Dorchester, Shrewsbury, and Exeter formed the original Dorchester
Company to exploit the Council's patent for fishing at Cape Ann. The
Reverend John White proved to be the most influential member of the
company, for he persuaded it to organize a permanent colony at Cape
Ann. Yet, in spite of repeated shipments of men and supplies, the colony
was a financial loss. In 1625 Roger Conant was put in charge. His first
problem was the claim of the Plymouth colony to the fishing and hunting rights in the area, a problem that was resolved when the Pilgrims
transferred their endeavors to the Kennebec. Not so readily solved were
problems such as the Cape's distance from good fishing banks and the
refusal of the men to produce some of the necessities of life. A year later
Conant led the remnants of the colony—some thirty men, women, and
children, from Cape Ann to the Naumkeag peninsula (now Salem).

Meanwhile, in England the Reverend Mr. White had changed the focus of the company from fishing to religion. While Conant struggled to
hold the small band together, White enlisted Puritan support to found a
colony for spreading the Puritan gospel. He and his supporters put their
sights on the patent of the old Dorchester Company, petitioning the

Council early in 1628 to allow them to assume the patent as the New England Company. The framers of the new patent knew little of the geography of New England and defined the company's limits as running from three miles north of the Merrimack River to three miles south of the Charles River, and inland to the Western Ocean. Later, boundary disputes between New Hampshire and Massachusetts were to develop from the vague wording that defined the company's northern limit. Typically, the grant infringed on other grants of the Council, such as the one to Mason and Gorges.

John Endecott was chosen as manager of the grant, and in June 1628 he and forty colonists set out for Naumkeag to prepare for future arrivals. With Endecott on his way, the new company made plans to obtain a royal charter. Supported by powerful nobles such as the Earl of Warwick and Lord Dorchester and by wealthy Londoners such as Mathew Cradock and Sir Richard Saltonstall, the New England Company received a royal charter in early March 1629, which created the Massachusetts Bay Company.

As soon as the company was officially organized, five ships filled with settlers, cattle, and agricultural implements sailed for Naumkeag. There they joined the small colony begun by Endecott along the South River, which was to become the principal harbor for Salem. (On the north side of the peninsula, the "old settlers" under Conant continued to reside apart.) Houses were built and crops planted nearby. Fishing was pursued with vigor to supply food for the settlers and for export. Cattle and goats were turned out to forage; the numerous salt and fresh-water marshes provided grasses and hay for the beasts. Shipbuilding had been started by carpenters sent over with Endecott, and ships would shortly become one of the coast's most important manufactures. Yet the arrival of several hundred new emigrants severely taxed the resources of the peninsula, where arable land was limited and shelter inadequate.[3] Better sites for agriculture lay some distance inland from the village and to the north or south along the coast, and small groups of settlers began to move to those sites.

Back in England significant changes in the structure of the Massachu-

3. Among the arrivals of the 1629 fleet were clergymen who founded the first church in America based on Puritan dogma, thus beginning at Salem the theocratic structure of later town settlement and governance throughout much of southern New England. Because the Puritan theocracy of seventeenth-century New England has been a subject of much research and writing and is not immediately geographic, the topic will not be discussed in this book, except in those instances where it directly influences the unfolding geographic patterns of the region.

setts Bay Company were taking place. A group of East Anglian Puritans, including the Earl of Lincoln, John Winthrop, Sr., and Isaac Johnson (Lincoln's brother-in-law) proposed to the Company that leading Puritans be invited to join in the emigration to New England. The Company's president, Mathew Cradock, in turn suggested that the governance of the colony be turned over to the settlers under conditions that would minimize control from London. In late August 1629 twelve Puritan leaders, including John Winthrop, Richard Saltonstall, Thomas Dudley, and William Pynchon, met secretly at Cambridge, where they pledged to move to the new colony if the Company would surrender to them all legal authority and the charter for transfer to New England. The intent was to free the colony from the interference of the royal government, its courts, and the bishops of the Church of England. This novel proposal was accepted, and in the fall of 1629 Winthrop was elected president. The Bay Company was now fully committed to the establishment of a Puritan state in New England. The winter was spent organizing the emigration, and on March 29, 1630, seven ships carrying the Company's new president, its council, and its charter, plus nearly a thousand settlers and their effects, left Southampton for Salem. Thus began the Puritan Great Migration to New England, which continued for a decade. Before the year's end, seventeen ships had followed in the wake of Winthrop's fleet.

Nearly a thousand English men, women, and children arrived on the shores of New England during the first wave of emigration. As a group they differed significantly from their Pilgrim predecessors, and in more than numbers: they were a composite of English society of the time, lacking only representatives of the poorest classes. Even nobility was represented—Deputy Governor Dudley was a member of a noble household, and Isaac Johnson was connected to a noble family by marriage. John Winthrop, Sr., was of the landed gentry, and the urban middle-class and mercantile interests of London were represented by men such as Sir Richard Saltonstall. Below in rank and status were the hundreds of yeomen, artisans, and laborers whose dissatisfaction with the England of Charles I sent them to a new life in New England. Religion was the most cohesive bond among the disparate social and economic backgrounds of the immigrants, for most of the party were Puritan or nonconformists of some degree. Among the leaders a large percentage had attended universities. The professions, such as law and the ministry, were represented. Although the immigrants came from all regions of

England, East Anglian non-conformists were probably the largest single element by regional origin, especially among the officials and clergymen. The beginnings of a *new* England were laid by a diverse and committed population.

Like other Englishmen of the time, the migrating Puritans had perceived their new homeland with a mixture of fact and fancy. Misconceptions—such as the belief that New England was a large island, that its streams rose in Lake Champlain, that the Western Ocean was not far off—were widely held, and knowledge gained from exploration only very slowly laid these notions to rest. The Puritans thought of New England as a spiritual desert, but they did not necessarily perceive the area as physically desolate and bleak. On the strength of the migration itself, one must conclude that the Puritans never doubted that New England could sustain them, although reservations about the wisdom of the regional choice lingered and were voiced openly during the Commonwealth in the suggestion that the colonists remove to Jamaica or another Caribbean island. New England might have been the choice simply because the Puritan leaders had obtained title to the area from the old Dorchester patent, but those leaders were too shrewd and too powerful to have acquiesced to New England had any significant doubts existed about their ability to live there. Other lands considered more satisfactory could have been obtained. Fortunately southern New England proved to be habitable quickly enough, although the Puritans realized that development of its resources, to quote the Reverend John White, had to be "purchased with hard labour."

The evidence from the 1620s that Englishmen could live in New England was sufficient to convince the Puritan leaders that there was no need to seek elsewhere. The Pilgrim experience was proof that people other than fur traders or fishermen could survive. Reports of Puritan agents such as Endecott were encouraging. Francis Higginson and Thomas Graves, among the earliest Puritans to arrive at Salem, wrote rather blissfully of their experiences. They described the region as healthful, with fertile and bountiful soils which yielded large harvests and rich pasturage which fattened the imported herds. It was also accessible to rich fishing grounds. Later writers, such as William Wood and John Winthrop, Sr., repeated the descriptions of a bountiful and productive region where the toil of honest men was amply rewarded by nature. Long after the Great Migration had started, the Puritans continued to think of New England as a refuge for the preservation of the integrity of their gospel, as a place where each individual could test his belief, and as a fertile and productive land where the Puritans as a group with hard work could comfortably sustain themselves.

"Salem, where we landed, pleased us not." Thus Deputy Governor Dudley summed up the immigrants' reaction to the settlement Endecott had developed to receive the newcomers. Dudley did not say why Salem was disappointing, but he did note that it seemed incapable of providing for the hundreds of new arrivals. Soon after his arrival at Salem, John Winthrop, Sr., led a party to survey Boston Bay, which Francis Higginson had earlier described as having "as fat black earth as can be seen anywhere." Having explored the bay, its islands, and a short distance up both the Charles and Mystic rivers, Winthrop concluded that the immigrants should settle along the Mystic. Until that time, at least, the Puritan leadership had apparently wanted to keep the entire group together at one site, even though the Salem experience had indicated that few New England sites would be capable of supporting such a large number of people. Dudley challenged Winthrop's proposal, however, by offering an alternative site on the banks of the Charles River. A second exploring party agreed that Dudley's site was satisfactory; the offer, however, served only to prolong the arguments among the leadership rather than to resolve them. A temporary compromise site was selected at Charlestown (at the mouth of the Charles River), where a few colonists from Salem had already settled. There, in mid-June 1630, the settlers disembarked to await the final decision on the colonial site.

Meanwhile the Reverend John White (of the earlier Dorchester Company) had dispatched a shipload of settlers to Salem. These new arrivals, some 140 persons, intended to remain independent to the Winthrop group. They also sent a survey party into Massachusetts Bay, where they selected Mattapan peninsula as the site for their settlement, which they named Dorchester in honor of their home village in England.

Among the settlers at Charlestown, individual action began to replace group indecision. Small groups, each under the leadership of one or two prominent men, broke from the main body and began to establish separate settlements. In July 1630 Sir Richard Saltonstall and the Reverend Mr. Phillips led a party about a mile above Dudley's site on the Charles to found Watertown. William Pynchon led another group to found Roxbury, and a few families drifted to Winthrop's original choice on the Mystic to begin Medford. Some settlers, of course, chose to stay at Charlestown. Across the river from Charlestown was the Shawmut

Peninsula, where the Anglican minister, William Blackstone (Blaxton) had resided since the mid-1620s. He invited Isaac Johnson to be his guest; once one prominent leader was established in the household, others began to frequent the peninsula. Even Winthrop decided to make Shawmut his permanent residence, supposedly attracted by the presence of a spring. By September 1630 many others had followed him, making Shawmut the largest of the several communities around Massachusetts Bay. The peninsula was then renamed Boston. The concept of a unified colony was partially revived in December 1630 when the leaders, meeting at Watertown, agreed to move their residences to Newtown (later Cambridge), Dudley's site on the Charles. The agreement, however, did not require other settlers to follow, and the plan was never fulfilled. Thus by the fall of 1630, the Puritan colonists, busy with construction to protect themselves from the oncoming winter, were dispersed among seven communities: Salem on the north, Dorchester on the south, and between them Boston, Medford, Charlestown, Watertown, and Roxbury (see Fig. 1-3).

Suggested References

Andrews, Charles M. *The Colonial Period of American History.* 4 vols. (New Haven, Conn.: Yale University Press, 1934–38).

Baxter, James P. (ed.). *Sir Ferdinando Gorges and His Province of Maine.* 3 vols. (Boston: Prince Society, 1890).

Bradford, William. *History of Plymouth Plantation 1620–1647.* 2 vols. (Boston: Massachusetts Historical Society, 1912).

Dexter, H. M. (ed.). *Mourt's Relation or a Journal of the Plantation at Plymouth.* (Boston: John K. Wiggin, 1865).

Langdon, G. D. *Plymouth Colony: A History of New Plymouth 1620–1691* (New Haven, Conn.: Yale University Press, 1966).

McManis, Douglas R. "English Evaluation of North American Iron during the Late Sixteenth and Early Seventeenth Centuries" (*Professional Geographer,* XXI (March 1969), 93–96).

Morison, Samuel E. *Builders of the Bay Colony* (Boston: Houghton Mifflin, 1930).

Notestein, Wallace. *The English People on the Eve of Colonization 1603–1630* (New York: Harper and Brothers, 1954).

Pomfret, John E. *Founding the American Colonies 1583–1660* (New York: Harper and Row, 1970).

Rutman, Darrett B. "The Pilgrims and Their Harbor" (*William and Mary Quarterly*, 3rd Series, XVII (April 1960), 164–75).

Winthrop, John Sr. *Winthrop's Journal: History of New England, 1630–1649.* 2 vols. Ed. James K. Hosmer (New York: Barnes and Noble, 1966).

Young, Alexander (ed.). *Chronicles of the First Planters of the Colony of Massachusetts Bay* (Boston: Charles C. Little and James Brown, 1846).

3 SETTLEMENT AND DEMOGRAPHIC PATTERNS

After 1630 New England underwent an intensive period of Europeanization that successively transformed the indigenous landscape into one dominated by a population of European backgrounds. The settlements that had already been established became the starting points from which people and their ways of life spread throughout the region. At first the few coastal settlements in the region were but a small-scale England overseas, but in time the entire region became "new" England in fact as well is in name: English by heritage, yet by the end of the colonial period, a distinct regional complex ready to shed its political ties to the mother country. English precedents were the bases by which the immigrants had established themselves in the New World habitat. But those Old World ways-of-doing were almost immediately modified as the colonists adopted native practices or adjusted to local soils and climatic conditions. Modification of English behavior continued until a distinctive, non-English cultural geography existed in New England. The individuality of colonial development was encouraged by the selective transfer of English practices to the colonies and by the relative freedom (guaranteed by conditions of the times) from restraints of English traditions such as feudal rights and land entailments, from English local government, which was a combination of feudalism and later innovation, and from many contemporary actions of the central government that were reshaping the landscape of Britain. Faced with the challenges of a new habitat, the colonists generally used their English background as a guideline for their actions, but decisions determining spatial patterns in the new overseas settlements were made in the context of colonial well-being, and not England's, often to the distress of authorities in the mother country. Such divergence from English heritage was accentuated as native-born Americans gradually replaced English-born founders in the political, social, and economic structure of the colonies. Meanwhile, the colonial population increased and spread into new areas, a process which expanded the portion of New England being subjected to the processes of Europeanization. By the end of the seventeenth century, the results of those processes in the form of landscape change were readily visible.

Settlement

By 1630 three nuclei of English settlement, each with different characteristics, had been established on New England's east coast. On the south coast the Dutch were active as fur traders and had yet to establish their post at Hartford, but they had begun settlement on Long Island, which some New Englanders considered to be part of their region until Crown decree in the late-seventeenth century assigned the island to the province of New York. The northernmost nucleus included the colonies at the mouth of the Piscataqua River, as well as the fishing stations on the coast and the offshore islands. Perhaps several hundred people, all brought to the New World by economic motives, inhabited those scattered settlements. The southernmost nucleus, Plymouth, in the sense of a transfer of English society and continuous occupance, was the first permanent English settlement on the coast. After a decade of existence, during which time its population had risen to nearly 500 persons, it had become a near-subsistence agrarian community. But even then the village was experiencing a shortage of desired land types, and settlers were beginning to eye the vacant lands across the bay at Duxbury as a site for a new village. Economic activities other than farming were not enough to provide an alternative means of livelihood, so that the Pilgrims became the first of many New Englanders to use emigration to new lands as a solution to the local land-shortage problem. Their attempts at fishing had been unsuccessful, while the fur trade, successfully extended to the west of Cape Cod and to the Kennebec River, did not employ many men.

The Massachusetts Bay Colony, the middle nucleus, was to be dominant in the later development of New England. Then confined to seven settlements around Massachusetts Bay, the Puritans represented a broad spectrum of English society whose varied activities would shortly be the primary agents of geographic change. The most recent of the nuclei to be established, the Bay Colony was the terminus for the large numbers of people who emigrated from England between 1630 and 1640 (the "Great Migration"). The spread of immigrants from the Bay Colony throughout southern New England was one of the most important elements in the region's transformation. The dynamic growth of the Bay Colony and its rapid rise to regional supremacy contrasted with the slow progression of events in the other two nuclei.

The cluster of Puritan-dominated settlements around Massachusetts Bay became the principal center of English expansion throughout southern New England. Commercial interests, desire for more land, and political rivalries were all important motives in the colonists' dispersal from Massachusetts, but the outstanding motive between 1630 and 1640 lay in religious disputes among the Puritans, earlier an important factor in the breakdown of the original concept of a single settlement among the founders of the colony. Their migration from a realm of enforced religious authority had provided a model for future dissenters in the Bay Colony, and in 1636 Roger Williams, dissatisfied with the theocracy, left to establish a new settlement on the banks of a stream near its confluence with Narrangansett Bay. He named the settlement Providence. In 1638 Anne Hutchinson, focus of one of the most notorious colonial religious disputes, and her followers settled at Portsmouth on Aquidneck Island in Narragansett Bay. Their settlement was in turn racked by disputes, and part of the group withdrew to the southern end of the island, where Newport was founded in 1639. Grotonites, another group of Massachusetts dissenters, began Warwick, west of Providence on the mainland. Those four settlements, two on the mainland and two on the islands of Narragansett Bay, eventually federated as the colony of Rhode Island and Providence Plantation.

The Hutchinson dispute also sent religious emigrants northward. In 1639 Anne Hutchinson's brother-in-law, John Wheelwright, led a group to Exeter, New Hampshire, to escape persecution by Massachusetts authorities. The introduction of a group of religiously motivated emigrants among the commercially oriented residents of the Piscataqua area was to cause disputes to flare in later years, as the Puritan group tried to establish its hegemony over the province of New Hampshire.

Jealousies and rivalries among religious leaders and dissatisfaction with available lands in the Bay Colony caused others to emigrate to the Connecticut Valley. Descriptions of its large expanses of rich meadows and prolific fur-bearing animals had reached the coastal settlements from several sources. Rich lands outside the jurisdiction of the Bay Colony were a powerful inducement to men who resented the official theocracy but who, unlike Williams and Hutchinson, had not assumed religious positions that made them unacceptable to Puritan leadership. By 1636 emigrants from Dorchester, Watertown, and Cambridge had trekked overland on the Great Trail (an Indian pathway leading from the coast to the middle Connecticut Valley), settling Hartford, Windsor, and Wethersfield on the Connecticut River—the nucleus of the colony of Connecticut. The actions of the Cambridge emigrants illustrate the political maneuvers that preceded the migration to the Connecticut Valley and demonstrate the intertwining of motives that sparked the trek. A petition to the General Court (the colonial assembly of the Bay Colony) requesting permission to depart the Bay Colony stressed the lack of suitable land in Cambridge. The General Court's offers of alternative lands within the Colony were rejected by the group's leader, Thomas Hooker, who hoped to establish a personal ministerial fiefdom independent of the constraints of the Massachusetts theocracy. Since most of the lands offered were taken up by later settlers, there can be no doubt about their suitability for settlement, but the petitioners were not solely motivated by a desire for new lands. So Hooker's followers sold their lands in Cambridge to recent arrivals from England in what was to become a standard practice of continental westward movement for nearly three centuries—an early example of one wave of migration replacing another in the older settlements. At the same time that the three Connecticut River towns were being settled, William Pynchon led a group from Roxbury to Springfield—also on the Connecticut, but some distance to the north of the others. For a brief time Springfield was associated with them but eventually chose to remain part of Massachusetts, even though Pynchon soon ran afoul of the governing theocracy. He returned to England rather than abandon his beliefs.

Two other settlements had their origins in the reluctance of English emigrants to stay in the Puritan theocracy. Saybrook, at the mouth of the Connecticut River, was founded in 1634 by settlers who landed in Boston but quickly decided to settle elsewhere. Similarly, English emigrants under the leadership of John Davenport and Theophilus Eaton, two independent-minded Puritans, examined a few sites in the Bay Colony before taking their followers to the northern shores of Long Island Sound. Since they planned to live by trade, Davenport and Eaton selected a site near the mouth of the Quinnipiac River, where New Haven was founded in 1639. With the founding of New Haven the six settlement nodes of seventeenth-century New England had been created: coastal New Hampshire–Maine, Massachusetts Bay, Plymouth, Rhode Island and Providence Plantation, the towns on the Connecticut River, and New Haven.

The fur trade played an important role in the expansion of settlement throughout New England. Traders pushed into the wilderness well in advance of settlement, and in their search for pelts they explored areas known only to the Indians, returning with pelts and information about the geography and circulation patterns beyond the English settlements. Thus they prepared for the movement of permanent settlers. The information gathered by Plymouth traders who trapped the Connecticut Valley, Narragansett Bay, and the Kennebec Valley is a good example of how the fur trade contributed to the knowledge of an area before settlement. The reports of John Oldham, a Bay Colony trader, were instrumental in determining the sites of Hartford, Windsor, and Wethersfield in the Connecticut Valley. Captain Neale's report on the region west of the Piscataqua (occasioned by a search for the Lake of the Iroquois —really Lake Champlain displaced too far eastward on maps of the period—ordered by the Laconia Company in 1632) remained the basis of knowledge about the region for many years.

In New England the fur trade created no nodes of settlement as it did in French North America, but it was responsible for a few individual settlements. Some of the posts established by traders developed a more diversified base of activities; others, however, dwindled as the trade diminished. Fur trading played a small part in the founding of Concord in 1635, the first interior town in the Bay Colony. Lancaster and Chelmsford, founded in 1645 and 1652 respectively, were started as posts to insure a flow of pelts to Boston, and at mid-century, Sudbury, Groton, and Cambridge each had a small but active fur trade. In the Connecticut Valley William Pynchon set up a series of posts at valley sites and in the hills around Springfield, of which Westfield was the most important. More typical than posts dealing exclusively in furs, however, were the frontier settlements, where the trade was only one aspect of the economy. Northampton and other towns north of Springfield all had a representative of the Pynchon interests among their founders.

Expansion of English settlement in New England created not only new settlement nodes but also new towns within the original coastal nuclei. In a pattern somewhat analogous to Greek diffusion throughout the Mediterranean, a new town was often sponsored by an older one. That pattern was first demonstrated in New England at Plymouth when a group crossed the bay to found Duxbury. Although the mother town pattern was well defined by mid-seventeenth century, it should be noted that even then some towns were formed by gathering emigrants from more than one town. In later decades the relationship of new towns to older ones started to become obscure, as new towns often drew settlers from a variety of places. After the original splintering to Duxbury, land pressures in Plymouth continued, causing others to move to sites on Cape Cod. The same kind of pressure sent people westward and north-ward to lay out Taunton, Attleborough, Marshfield, and Scituate. As the filling-in process developed in the Bay Colony, the founding of Dedham, Sudbury, Mendon, Andover, and other towns marked the push of settle-ment in the interior, while the founding of Ipswich, Rowley, Hampton, Lynn, and Saugus spread contiguous settlement along the coast. Com-parable patterns of expansion took place in the Connecticut Valley, where Haddam, Middletown, and Farmington were founded as outliers of the three original river towns. To the north, the founding of Hadley, Northampton, Greenfield, and Deerfield carried out the pattern in the Massachusetts section of the Valley. Along Long Island Sound, satellites of both the Connecticut River towns and New Haven developed. Guil-ford, established in 1639, was the last settlement on the Sound made in-dependently of a colonial sponsor. New Englanders also spilled across the Sound to Long Island and established towns on its eastern end, much to the displeasure of the Dutch, who claimed the entire island and had begun settlement on its western end across from New Amsterdam (New York).

Demographic Patterns

In 1640 the basic settlement pattern of New England was based upon the six discrete nodes established in the preceding decades. Only one of those nodes—in the Connecticut Valley—was not coastal, but even it had fairly direct access to the sea. By 1660 creation of new towns had brought about coalescence of the three original coastal nuclei. Accord-ingly, a continuum of towns stretched from the southern end of Penobscot Bay (Maine) to Cape Cod. It included the settlements at Casco and Saco bays and York and Wells in southern Maine; the villages at the mouth of the Piscataqua and south along the coast to Cape Ann; the towns of the Massachusetts Bay Company; and Plymouth and the newer towns of Plymouth Colony. Only at two points had settlement limits pushed an appreciable distance from the ocean or tidal streams. Concord was no longer separated from the Bay node; it had become a westward projection of the node along the Sudbury River. Immediately to the south, Framingham and Dedham brought the southern fringe of the node inland. The second interior extension was in Plymouth, where a corridor of towns linked to those around Narragansett Bay, although settlement was still absent from the southwestern part of the colony.

Of the western nodes, only one had become directly linked to the original coastal nodes. The Connecticut River towns and New Haven were still separated from the nodes by unsettled territory, but expansion of the mainland towns on the northern shores of Narragansett Bay had met the westward spread of Plymouth. There still remained unsettled country west of Narragansett Bay which separated the Rhode Island towns from their nearest Connecticut neighbors. The colony of Connecticut in 1660 consisted of three discrete population units. The eastern unit centered on New London and extended inland northward along the Thames River and its tributaries. On Long Island Sound a contiguous group of towns ran from Saybrook to Greenwich, which bordered on New Netherland (New York). The original river towns and their newer satellites comprised the third unit. Further up the Connecticut Valley a large inland enclave existed between Springfield and Hadley, and two smaller enclaves were found between it and the Massachusetts Bay node. One included Groton and Lancaster, an outlier of the Concord–Sudbury projection. The other, Brookfield, was little more than a way-station on the Great Trail from the Bay settlements to towns on the Connecticut River.

On the eve of King Philip's War—the mid-1670s—there were no changes in basic settlement patterns from those observable in 1660 (see Fig. 3-1). Coalescence and movement into the interior were the trends reflected in the 1670 distribution of settlements and population. In the Bay Colony, settlement had spread to cover the eastern third of the province. The towns of northern Rhode Island and eastern Connecticut had been linked. Along Long Island Sound, towns stretched in an unbroken line from Westerly, Rhode Island, to Greenwich, Connecticut;

SETTLED AREAS OF NEW ENGLAND

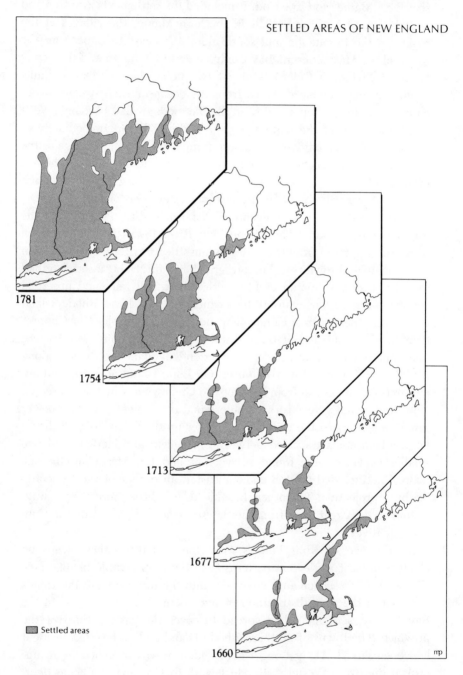

1781

1754

1713

1677

1660

Settled areas

mp

Figure 3-1.

in the Connecticut Valley from Saybrook, Connecticut, to Hadley, Massachusetts. Brookfield remained an isolated outlier, as did Deerfield and Northfield, then the northern limits of English settlement in the Valley. The Groton–Lancaster enclave had been absorbed into the Bay node, whose western limit was then at Worcester.

After King Philip's War the pattern was altered radically. Many settlements were attacked and destroyed by the Indians during the brief war; others were abandoned by the fear-stricken colonists. As a result the settlement area was smaller than it had been in 1660. Except in the Bay Colony's coastal node and along Long Island Sound west of the Connecticut River, where settlers had been least affected by the war, the frontier line had generally retreated. Except for Hatfield and Hadley, the Connecticut Valley north of Springfield was practically abandoned, as were the towns of Brookfield and Worcester. A small nucleus remained in eastern Connecticut around New London, Norwich, and Stonington, but the rest of eastern Connecticut and western Rhode Island was empty of English settlers. The town pattern that had once reached Penobscot Bay now ended at the mouth of the Piscataqua. From there a few scattered settlements bravely survived, but none beyond the estuary of the Kennebec River.

The colonists began the task of restoring settlements once King Philip's War had ended, but they had barely returned to the prewar status quo before the repeated devastations of the colonial wars with France began in the reign of William III. Once again the settled area drew together under the impact of Indian ravages in the countryside. The effect of King Philip's War on the settlement pattern of New England was only a foreshadow of the destruction that eighteenth-century warfare would inflict on the colonies. The spread of population to new areas was affected not only by the constant threat and occasional realization of warfare, but also by the fact that the remaining unsettled parts of New England had relatively small amounts of the types of land preferred by the colonists. Once better lands elsewhere became available, many settlers left the region. The nineteenth-century rural depopulation of New England had been anticipated.

By the early years of the eighteenth century, unsettled areas were to be found only in western and northern New England; thus areas into which population could expand were all part of the buffer zone between the English and French cores of settlement where the intermittent warfare of the century was waged. Advance of the frontier occurred chiefly during the intervals between the colonial wars. In the eighteenth century the process of expansion became a continuum, in direct contrast to the seventeenth-century process, which was marked by migration across unsettled wilderness to areas of preferred land types, where discrete population nuclei were established. By the eve of the French and Indian War, the frontier line had advanced on the northeast to the eastern side of the Penobscot estuary, inland along the Kennebec, and behind the older towns south of Saco Bay. In New Hampshire, settlement had advanced up the Merrimack River and extended into the region between the river and the old coastal towns. The aggressive promotional policies of that colony had resulted in the creation of settlements in the south central portion of the colony and in the repopulation of the Connecticut Valley immediately north of the New Hampshire–Massachusetts line. In Massachusetts most of Worcester County had been settled, and a continuous grouping of towns stretched inland to the towns of the Connecticut Valley. There towns had been re-established and new ones had developed, creating a contiguous pattern of settlement from the river's mouth into southern New Hampshire and Vermont. Even though the colonists had barely begun to penetrate the Berkshire Hills, a series of new towns had been established on the western flank of the hills in the Housatonic Valley. Litchfield County in northwestern Connecticut had been divided into towns and settlements begun. Similarly, the remaining unsettled parts of northeastern Connecticut had been divided into towns, so that no large areas of that colony remained undivided or unsettled. When the colonial wars ended, only in Maine (then owned by Massachusetts) and New Hampshire were there large expanses still to be populated; Vermont, however, remained virtually unsettled.

After the close of the French and Indian War, when the threat of warfare was finally removed from New England, the expansion process regained momentum. Before the Revolutionary War, settlement in Maine had pushed eastward from the Pensumpscot River to the St. Croix; a series of towns stretched up the Kennebec as far as Madison, and in the lower Androscoggin Valley, settlements testified to the general inland thrust of colonists once the end of warfare had created a sense of security. But in terms of area brought into settlement between the end of the imperial wars and the beginning of the Revolution, the renewed settlement momentum was most evident in New Hampshire. By the opening of the Revolution only the northernmost quarter of that province remained unpopulated, for settlers had quickly spread into the central parts of the colony, pushing northward beyond the head of the Merrimack. New Hampshire's aggressive promotional land policies had not only created towns in the eastern side of the upper Connecticut Valley but had also spread settlers into adjoining parts of Vermont on land claimed by both New Hampshire and New York. Settlement had been initiated in southwestern Vermont from New York, so that colonists were found throughout the disputed area on both sides of the Green Mountains.

The newly opened lands must certainly have disappointed the settlers, for instead of finding more of New England's prized land types, they found those least suited to agriculture. The extremely rough hills of northern New England, such as the Green or White mountains, which in the fashion of the times the settlers called mountains, contained only small pockets of land suitable for cropping in the narrow U-shaped valleys that cut through the hills. In a region generally characterized by hilly, rough terrain and thin, rocky soils, the narrow upper Connecticut Valley and the broad Champlain lowland stood out as exceptions; there terrain and soils were more comparable to those of southern New England. But even so, the amount of tillable land was limited; in addition these areas came with the additional liability of a considerably more severe climate, with a shorter growing season and intense winters with heavy snowfalls.

While physical conditions restricted the agricultural potential of the newly settled regions, increased distances from the established centers placed limitations on economic development. Few of those regions were accessible to markets by navigable streams. Only the Connecticut, Kennebec, Androscoggin, and Merrimack rivers were navigable; areas not immediately adjacent to them had to rely on land transportation for their connections to New England's marketplaces. But links to markets were only one aspect of the problems faced by the frontiersmen. The frontier itself was nearly self-sufficient in foodstuff supply, thus local markets were almost non-existent for a frontier farmer. The urban centers in the older settled areas of New England were experiencing little or no population increase, so that they were not real market areas for the frontier produce. Also, those centers had long before established food-supply linkages with adjacent tributary areas or had become dependent on foodstuffs imported from the Middle Colonies. Thus, even if transportation links had existed between the urban centers and the frontier, the market for the settlers' products would have been negli-

gible. Unable to produce large amounts of marketable agricultural surplus, encumbered by transport problems, and burdened by high land
costs and the aftermath of wartime financial policies, new settlements in
the eighteenth century were not as quickly absorbed by the commercial
system of the region as most new settlements had been in the seventeenth
century.

The transition from a settlement policy to a speculative land policy,
which took place in the early years of the eighteenth century, had noticeable consequences on frontier development. The ability to purchase
land became a major factor in migration, and the homogeneous pattern
of townspeople migrating as a group to the wilderness broke down.
Group migration did not cease entirely, but movements of individual
families began to account for a greater proportion of frontier migration.
Speculators usually divided their towns into regular geometric units.
This resulted in an initially dispersed population pattern, a significant
contrast to the nucleation during the frontier phase in the older settled
areas. Settlement dependent on ability to purchase land tended to create a more socially diverse population on the frontier, but it also placed
on the new settlers financial burdens unknown to their counterparts of
earlier days.

While most New Englanders seeking new land stayed within the region, either taking up farms in the less satisfactory parts of the older
settlements or tying their fates to the more restricted opportunities of
the frontier, others decided to seek more attractive lands elsewhere. The
consequence was a return to the early dispersal pattern of New England
settlement; the crucial variation was that the lands to which they migrated were outside New England. During the nineteenth century that
process would spread large numbers of New Englanders throughout the
United States. At first, however, the renewed process involved only a
small number of people, and the range of migration was restricted to
counties in New York adjoining Connecticut and to northern New Jersey, where New Englanders had arrived as early as the 1660s. More ven-
turesome pioneers moved to South Carolina (Colleton County) and
Medway, Georgia, while others, such as the Scotch–Irish migrants from
Londonderry, New Hampshire, pioneered the Cherry Valley, the first
penetration of New Englanders into the upper Susquehanna area. After
mid-eighteenth century a substantial number of New Englanders migrated to Nova Scotia.

A prelude to the large-scale emigration from the region after the Revolutionary War was the transfer of hundreds of New Englanders to the Delaware and Susquehanna valleys of northern Pennsylvania. Sponsored by land companies formed in Connecticut and founded on land claimed by the terms of that colony's charter, the Pennsylvania settlements began to appear in the early 1760s. By the eve of the Revolution hundreds of families had moved to the area. Those frontier settlements, like comparable ones in New England, were subjected to Indian harassment and ravages during the Revolution and were temporarily abandoned after two barbarous massacres: one in the Wyoming Valley, the other in the Cherry Valley. At the end of the war many settlers returned, but by that time the range of New Englanders' emigration had expanded to encompass the entire American frontier as it spread westward across the continent.

THE TOWN SYSTEM

The expansion of New England's six population-political nodes was accomplished by the town system. In contrast to the rest of the United States, where the word *town* describes a small urban center such as a village or small city, a town in New England is a large tract of land with defined legal status, privileges, and responsibilities—a minor civil division, which elsewhere in the country would be called a township. The use of the word is not only unique to New England, but the land system in which the town was the basic component gave distinctive characteristics to the landscape of New England not found in the other seaboard colonies. Initially a town was assigned to a group of settlers; thus settlement in colonial New England was predominantly a group action. The solitary individual or family pushing into the wilderness, so romanticized in later American frontier mythology, was generally absent from New England—at least until the pattern of group migration began to weaken somewhat by the middle of the eighteenth century. Interestingly enough, as group migration was ebbing within New England, it remained the basis of emigration from the region. Bands of New Englanders, in some instances all of them from the same town, left their native region in search of better fortune; the family that left New England unescorted by other families was a great rarity. And scions of those transplanted New Englanders also seemed to prefer the group-migration pattern in new cycles of exodus to western lands, a pattern that persisted into the nineteenth century. An important consequence of the town system as the principal means of settlement expansion was the creation of communities in various degrees of nucleation. The system provided many benefits to the colonists. Because of the close proximity of families, it virtually enforced cooperation among settlers, ensuring concern for the common as well as the individual good. Tools and equipment could be shared; community tasks such as fence and road building could proceed with some order. Disputes could be resolved by a central authority. Town meetings provided opportunity for citizens to participate in the running of local affairs. Because the town was the legal creation of a provincial government, land titles were regularized, and the social character of the settlement monitored. However, dissident beliefs and uncivil behavior arose in spite of efforts to control and patrol, so that the maximum effectiveness of the system rarely was achieved except in times of extreme crisis. Still, as a medium of settlement expansion and as a means of spatial organization, the town system was a success and continued to be used in later centuries in spite of its weaknesses.

In the past the New England town has been studied mainly as a political religious, or social institution. Here it is proposed to conceive of it spatially, as a collection of communities. A town had its beginnings when a group of people petitioned the ruling colonial body to establish a new settlement, which was a plantation until it was officially granted town status. If that body was agreeable to the petition, a tract for the new settlement was delimited and a committee of proprietors appointed to handle the tasks of initial settlement. The proprietors made arrangements for migration to the new area, determined the site for the house lots, and decided how land was to be distributed among the settlers and how fields were to be utilized. In many instances they even arranged to have shelters built before the families migrated. In most towns the original proprietary committee later gave way to town meetings and elected officials. When the settlement was well established, it was raised by assembly action from a plantation to town status; town status, among other things, required the community to support a church and a minister and to send representatives to the colonial assembly. The problem of obtaining land titles from the Indians was usually the responsibility of the central colonial government, following the precedent of the Bay Colony, which in 1635 forbade individual acquisitions from the tribes and made its General Court the sole dispenser of legal titles within the colony. Within a town, transfer of title to individuals remained a matter of local decision. The conventions of English land tenure were the usual guidelines followed in land-divisions, but, because English precedents varied, land-allotment patterns differed among the towns, dependent on the previous experience of leaders and the objectives of the proprietors.

The tracts assigned to a new plantation varied in size and shape, but they always contained more than enough land to maintain the first settlers and their families. Dedham, with its original tract of nearly 200 square miles, was probably uniquely large, even in an era when boundaries of grants were imprecise. Watertown's initial size is difficult to determine, but original grants in the town accounted for more than 29,000 acres. Sudbury, founded in 1638, contained more than 20,000 acres. Andover initially had about 60 square miles. Inevitably each town included several different types of land: meadow, usually in a stream bottom or adjoining a pond, marsh, or swamp; timbered land, sometimes with cleared areas that were the result of Indian burning practices; and rocky, timbered uplands. The tracts were normally a compact unit. Boston, however, had special problems, the result of limited space and sparse timber on its small peninsula, and was given non-contiguous tracts. Braintree and Muddy River (Brookline) were added to the town of Boston to provide agricultural lands, and Noodle Island was assigned for timber.

Within the plantation the center of activities was the site selected for the house lots. A lot was assigned to each family for house, garden, and storage buildings. In coastal towns the house-lot tracts usually were located close to the harbor. In the interior towns many variables—such as available surface water, amount of level terrain, nearness to meadows and fields, possibility of flood damage, and presence of forest clearings determined the location of the residential nucleus. An Indian clearing located on a terrace above the river bottom spared the toil of clearing the forest, placed the settlers close to their fields and meadows, and removed dwellings from the dangers of all but the highest floods. The size of individual house lots differed among the towns, although four to six acres seemed to be a frequently allotted unit during the seventeenth century. Parcels of that size permitted houses to be relatively close together with enough remaining land for gardens, barns, and animal runs. One of several exceptions, however, was Waterbury, Connecticut. There, house lots of eight acres each were initially planned, but the size was eventually reduced to two acres. Social status and wealth were important in determining the size of a family's lot; indeed, in some towns these factors were more significant than need. During the eighteenth century, as the shape of towns became more geometrically regular, the size and

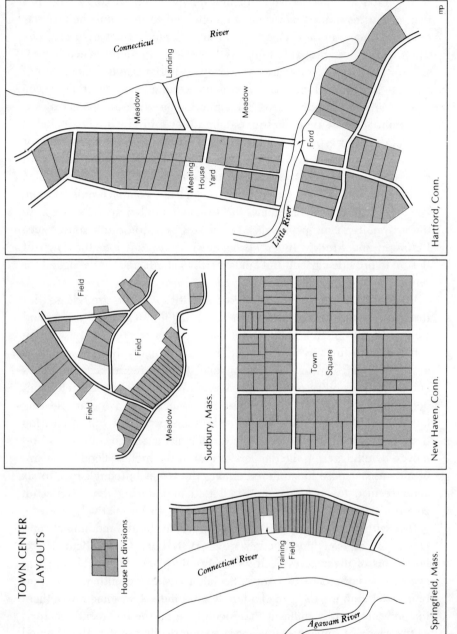

TOWN CENTER
LAYOUTS

House lot divisions

Hartford, Conn.

Sudbury, Mass.

New Haven, Conn.

Springfield, Mass.

Connecticut   River
Landing
Meadow   Meadow
Ford
Meeting
House
Yard
Little River

Field
Field
Field
Field
Meadow

Town
Square

Connecticut River
Training
Field
Agawam River

Figure 3-2.

shape of house lots tend to become more uniform, although rich settlers or proprietors could always obtain larger units than those of their co-townsmen.

The shape of an individual lot was usually rectangular, although square lots were not uncommon. In some places such as Springfield, Massachusetts, long, narrow lots ran from a central street to the river's edge, producing a pattern comparable to the seigneurial subdivisions of the lower St. Lawrence Valley and indeed to many other areas of colonial settlement. Where the terrain did not permit compact geometric lots, asymmetrical forms appeared along the streets or paths that wound among marshes, ponds, coastal inlets, and rock outcrops. Although the shape and size of the lots determined whether the houses and other structures were close together or spread apart, a dispersed or concentrated residential housing pattern in any town involved other factors as well, among them being the desire of town and provincial religious leaders to keep their "flocks" closely knitted and supervised or to maintain the residential layouts that they had known in England.

Like other features of early settlement, the plan for the house-lots tract varied from town to town (see Fig. 3-2), but a common layout placed the lots on each side of a central street. The description of early Providence as "houses scattered along a crooked path" was true of many other villages of the era. This arterial plan was one of the prevailing forms in the Connecticut Valley, well suited to the narrow riverine terraces. Also widely used was a rectangular layout, in which several streets or paths crossed each other at right angles or as the terrain demanded. New Haven's house-lot tract, an early example of the use of a rigid geometrical grid, was a large square subdivided into smaller squares, each a unit of town government. Waterbury was plotted in the same way, but the execution of the plan was less rigid. Normally, an area within each house-lots tract was reserved for public use. At first only a meeting house occupied the public area, but later jails, stocks, and fortified structures were built there.

In most towns the house lots comprised the initial community and served as the town center, or village. But enough examples of multinodal towns exist to eschew the generalization that all towns had only one center. Salem in the Massachusetts Bay Colony began as a dual-community town, one group on the north side of the peninsula, another (the more important one) on the south side. Hartford, Connecticut, was also composed of two communities: the settlers arriving in 1635 located

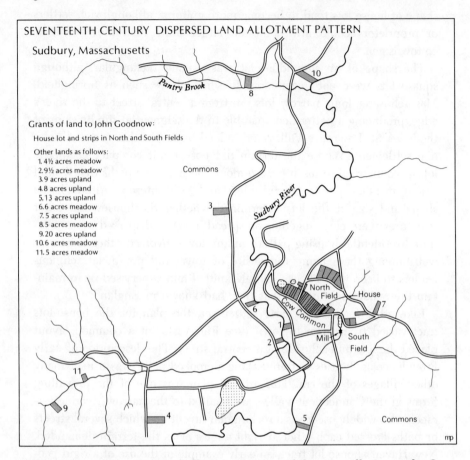

Figure 3-3. (From *Puritan Village* by Sumner Chilton Powell, Copyright ©
1963 by Wesleyan University Press, by permission)

north of Little River, and the 1636 arrivals located south of it. The two
groups were separated only by a short distance and a ford, yet they held
individual meetings and kept separate records for some years. At New
Haven two concentrations of houses developed outside the original village plot and were appropriately called "The Suburbs." Significantly, because they were not among the original proprietors of the town, the
"suburban" householders were denied the rights of townsmen for some
years. Many Connecticut Valley towns, such as Springfield and Hatfield,
acquired secondary villages when settlement sprang up on the bank opposite the original settlement.

Because of the large size of most original towns, the lands outside the village plot were rarely transferred to private ownership immediately after settlement. Watertown, Massachusetts, was a notable exception to that practice, for the entire town was allotted to the original colonists immediately after their arrival. In most towns the unallotted land passed into private ownership through a series of divisions. A settler might find his total acreage spread in several parcels around the village plot (see Fig. 3-3). Such dispersal meant that work was increased by time spent traveling from field to field, but each family's need for parcels of various types of land was met. The dispersed-holding pattern, which was familiar to many early settlers because it was similar to the feudal three-field holding system they had known in England, assured each family meadow for pasture, fields for crops, and upland tracts for timber.

Land tenure differed considerably from England, where most of the emigrants had been tenants. In New England, allotted lands were owned outright, without any vestige of feudalism such as the quit-rent system practiced in Maryland or Pennsylvania. Yet restrictions on private property rights were instituted in a few towns. Sudbury, Massachusetts, for example, established an open-field system in which private rights were restricted on certain communally owned and managed properties; thus anyone assigned to a common field found it necessary to cooperate with his neighbors on matters of crops, planting time, and harvest, if the system were to operate smoothly. But the system sometimes broke down, bringing out the worst in human nature as arguments over division of harvest or amount of working time arose. By the end of the seventeenth century the open-field system was rarely found in the new towns and was disappearing from the older ones. In order to preserve their original character, some towns decreed restrictions on sales of land to outsiders. In the long run such limitations laws were unenforceable, although efforts to restrict newcomers' participation in town government and in later land divisions continued well into the eighteenth century and were the sources of much social and political unrest. Unallocated land remained in common under the supervision of the town government, which also decided when and how it was to be transferred into private ownership. The commons consisted of two categories: public lands that were retained for community use and idle lands that were ultimately divided and allotted to individuals.

The dispersed land-holding pattern created by the early land divisions was the source of two trends crucial to later town development in New England: (1) it encouraged members of the community to consolidate

their holdings, and (2) it spurred farmers to move from the village plot
to locations closer to their fields. Secondary divisions of land distant
from the plot accentuated the latter trend, especially when the land was
bestowed on men with the wherewithal to consolidate and add to their
holdings and with the courage to defy local or provincial regulations.
Such rules required everyone to live within a half mile of the town
meetinghouse; scions of the town fathers often found it preferable to
move away in order to establish households independent of their
parents.

Many a New England farmer found the dispersed-field pattern an in-
convenience, even though paths soon led from the village plot to all
major fields. The distances separating fields from village could be considerable, and, in order to cut down on the time spent traveling among
the fields, a farmer might put up a shed for tools, animals, or crop storage at a convenient point along one of the paths. Later he might convert
it into a shelter for himself and other men who worked in the neighborhood but lived in the village. Finally he would build a substantial house
for himself and his family and move out of the village entirely. When
farms were established on distant, newly allocated land, however, the
families often migrated from the village to homestead in one step.

In an effort to retain control in the settlements, the colonial governments passed laws requiring all dwellings to be within a certain distance
of the meetinghouse—laws often justified on grounds of defense as the
theocratic structure broke down; such laws, however, were generally ignored by the townsmen and ultimately proved unenforceable. Thus outlying farms gradually became a characteristic of the town landscape, although their inhabitants retained important political ties with the town
center and continued to be dependent upon its church, school, and commercial establishments. The developing outlying communities fell into
one of two spatial patterns: some homesteads were grouped closely together to form a loosely nucleated hamlet, while others were dispersed
along paths or roadways widely separated from each other by farmlands.

Activities other than farming drew people away from the town center.
Gristmills and sawmills were erected at sites where waterpower was
available—usually in the physically rougher parts of a town, where little
farming was practiced. Trading posts—sometimes present before the settlers—and iron forges and furnaces also drew small communities around
them. The process of population dispersal throughout the town was not
a speedy one, but eventually it created conditions that challenged the

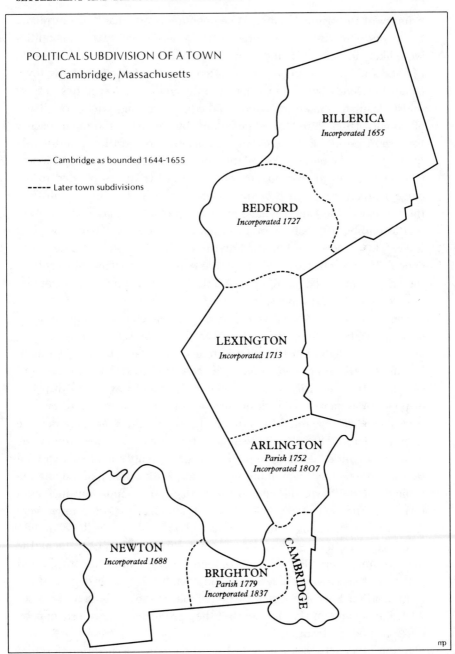

POLITICAL SUBDIVISION OF A TOWN
Cambridge, Massachusetts

——— Cambridge as bounded 1644-1655

----- Later town subdivisions

BILLERICA
Incorporated 1655

BEDFORD
Incorporated 1727

LEXINGTON
Incorporated 1713

ARLINGTON
Parish 1752
Incorporated 1807

NEWTON
Incorporated 1688

BRIGHTON
Parish 1779
Incorporated 1837

CAMBRIDGE

mp

Figure 3-4.

primacy of the original center. When enough people had been attracted to an outlying district, disagreements between the two communities were likely to arise, starting a new phase of relationships within a town. Members of the outer community often resented traveling to the town center to attend church and school and demanded such facilities in their midst. At first, complaints were handled by granting winter privileges of absence from church attendance and by "lending" the town teacher for a short period. But such compromises proved short-lived and inadequate. When the outlying population had increased sufficiently, the new community, with the permission of the parent village, separated to become a precinct or parish of the original town. Eventually, again with the consent of the parent village and with the authorization of the colonial assembly, a parish or precinct could be declared an independent town. This process of town subdivision (see Fig. 3-4) operated well enough for several decades, but by the end of the seventeenth century, the original towns began to oppose bitterly further reduction of population, territory, and revenues.

The model of the New England town as a collection of communities is as appropriate to the eighteenth century as to the seventeenth century, although the model must be altered to accommodate change. The number and population of communities in each town tended to increase. But as spatial fragmentation of both communities and towns and dispersal of population more evenly throughout the towns became more marked trends, the area occupied by individual communities tended to become more restricted. Thus the eighteenth-century town was characterized by more communities, each more populous but encompassing less area than seventeenth-century communities. Further, with spread of population throughout the town, the percentage of dispersed population increased relative to the nucleated portions. Population changes in the town were associated with changes in other spatial patterns as well. Churches, meetinghouses, and general stores, formerly found exclusively in the town centers were now apt to be found along connecting roads and paths, or at crossroads corners, reflecting again the greater degree of decentralization. Such changes were taking place in towns both in the older settled areas and on the frontier, but they produced a more pronounced difference on the frontier.

In the older settled areas, towns were no longer a medium of settlement. They had become instead the primary internal civil divisions of the colonies. Changing religious attitudes had lessened the importance of the town as a religious unit; indeed, with the decline of theocratic government and the spread of non-Puritan, Protestant groups, such as the Quaker, Baptist, and Anglican sects, religious uniformity throughout a town became a thing of the past. The subdivision of the older towns tended to make their sizes and shapes more uniform than they had been in the seventeenth century. General population increase and decreased acreages available for farms resulted in land pressures that brought many acres of non-preferred lands into productive use. Unallotted lands were converted to private ownership wherever possible, the values of pre-ferred land types rose sharply, and New Englanders in the older towns found that they could obtain land only through purchase, rent, or in-heritance. Further, agriculture had become less renumerative, for rea-sons which will be discussed in the next chapter. Except for periods of war, when demands and prices for agricultural commodities were in-flated, the general comparative position of New England agriculture was less favorable than for the other colonial regions. Plant diseases and misuse of the soil made the production of the most saleable crops impos-sible. The larger urban centers now depended on imported foodstuff rather than production from their immediate hinterlands and, although animal husbandry retained some measure of prosperity, the general status of New England agriculture was static, offering little hope of ma-terial improvement to farmers.

EIGHTEENTH-CENTURY FRONTIER TOWNS

In certain aspects the town of the eighteenth century was reminiscent of the original seventeenth-century model. On the frontier, towns continued to be the principal means of population expansion into unsettled areas, for few people wished to risk settlement in a new area until a town was laid out. The late seventeenth-century pattern of town design remained strongly entrenched, particularly in Maine and parts of New Hampshire, where Massachusetts was an active promoter of new settlements. The original scheme for Penacook (Concord), New Hampshire, provided for a town center of contiguous house lots along both sides of a central street with farmlands in several parcels around the center. Similarly, a closely nucleated village was planned for New Marblehead and Narragansett #1 (Buxton) in Maine. But even such planned retentions of traditional town features were unable to withstand the process of dispersal, and after a survey in 1759 the proprietors of New Marblehead dropped their efforts to keep the village as the town's central node of settlement. A re-

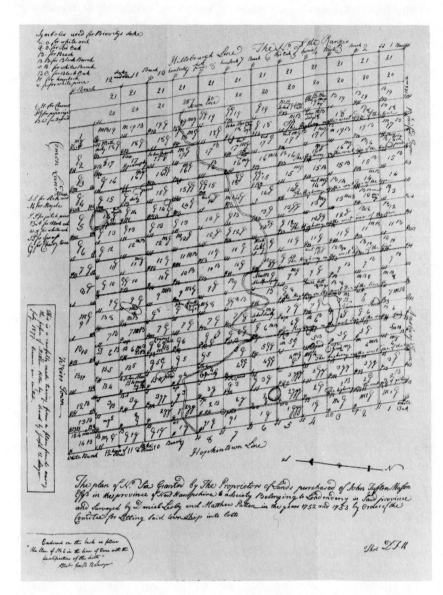

Figure 3-5. Eighteenth-Century Town Survey with no Town Center: Henniker, New Hampshire. (*New Hampshire Historical Society*)

cent historian of the Maine frontier concludes that settlers considered compact villages necessary only in times of danger, and that even then they preferred the haven of a stockade or garrison house to a village, where one had to live close to his neighbor and far from his fields.

Yet in other ways, the frontier towns of the eighteenth century were different from their predecessors. The spread of people throughout a town was more often the function of the initial layout, the proprietors' designs, or the immigrants' desire for consolidated holdings than the result of a long-term process of decentralization. For example, in New Hampshire at Londonderry or Bedford many of the original arrivals could not be accommodated at a single locale (in much the same way that Salem was unable to handle the large numbers of Puritans arriving in 1630), so they moved on, forming a dispersed pattern. In Henniker, New Hampshire, the town proprietors from the start admitted that decentralization was the spirit of the times and purposively omitted a town center from the initial survey of the town, allowing settlers to establish nodes wherever they found it most convenient (see Fig. 3-5). Thus, with the dispersal of people throughout the countryside and with fewer farmers living in the town centers, many eighteenth-century New England villages began to function as central places,[1] villages that bore little resemblance to semi-agricultural medieval hamlets that they had once been.

Another important determinant of the character of frontier towns during the eighteenth century was a shift of land-grant policy. In Massachusetts, Connecticut, and New Hampshire,[2] land grants were made largely to speculators, individuals, or groups to whom the province was indebted—people who had no intention of settling the land—rather than to individual or group petitioners whose main purpose was settlement. Of that critical change, historian Richard Hofstader wrote: "The urge to exploit the land was changing the old order, the Yankee enterpreneur was replacing the Puritan villager." One feature of the new policy was the division of huge tracts of land into towns of uniform size and geometric shape, distinctly different from the piecemeal pattern of the previous century but very similar to the rectangular grid survey used by the federal government west of the Appalachians in the post-Revolutionary

1. Central places are sites where non-agricultural activity is concentrated, where administrative, commercial, and professional services and other non-agricultural activities tend to cluster together because of vital linkages between them.
2. All land in Rhode Island had been allocated by mid-century.

period. This more rigidly geometric pattern may be seen today in the towns of the Connecticut Valley north of the Massachusetts–New Hampshire boundary, in Litchfield County, Connecticut, and in adjoining sections of western Massachusetts. Many towns in central New Hampshire were thus laid out, and the pattern is still apparent in the towns around Casco and Saco bays in Maine, which were created by the government of Massachusetts after 1713.

Speculative motives also influenced the internal division of new towns. As many original surveys indicate, the first concern of the proprietors was to dispose of land for a profit. They divided their towns into compact, saleable units—apparently with little concern for the settlers' needs. Most of the speculative towns did not retain large acreages of common lands for community use or later allotments, and any unsold land remained the property of the town proprietors rather than the settlers. Land acquisition depended on an individual's ability to purchase; it was not a social right, coming from his membership in a group, as it had been in the seventeenth century. Thus, the patchwork-quilt pattern of dispersed holdings of the early New England towns failed to reappear on the eighteenth-century frontier and compact farm units became the dominant feature of the rural landscape. Because some town designs did not include provisions for a town center, or because townsmen under threat of war often considered a stockade, garrison house, or fort the appropriate structure for the town center, the church or meetinghouse was forced to another location.

In spite of the detached relationship that the speculative proprietors assumed toward the new settlements, group settlement remained an important, if not exclusive, means to populate new towns, just as it had in the older ones. Group settlement for New Englanders was more than a tradition; it was a proved way of surviving on the frontier. Recognizing this, the speculators often organized groups to migrate to the new towns. A semblance of the older, mother-town pattern, in which an older town sponsored the settlement of a new one, continued, as names such as New Marblehead or New Gloucester indicated. The retention of old patterns was most noticeable in Maine, where Massachusetts actually forced their preservation through the conditions of its land grants.

POPULATION

Population figures for colonial New England are estimates based on fragmentary sources such as town records, official reports, unofficial notices, ship passenger lists, and infrequent censuses. Efforts to reconcile such data have resulted in widely ranging estimates. Considerable research on early American demography is currently underway, but no conclusive estimates have been accepted for New England. For the purpose of consistency, the figures used here are taken from a single scheme. Table I contains the estimated colonial population figures and growth rate per decade for the region as a whole and for each colony. Consistent increase of population was a trend throughout the colonial period, the only exception being Rhode Island's loss during the decade of the Revolution. Massachusetts had the largest population of the region, and, for a brief period in the mid-seventeenth century, the largest population of the seaboard colonies.[3] Connecticut ranked second, although during the eighteenth century its numbers increased more rapidly than that of first-place Massachusetts. With the exception of New Hampshire, which alone had a single node of population, each of New England's colonies had a multinodal internal distribution of people. In Massachusetts the scattered initial settlements around Massachusetts Bay had consolidated into a single node by the end of the seventeenth century; a second node centered on Springfield had developed in the Connecticut Valley; and a third node included the settlements along the coast of Maine. Rhode Island was binodal: one cluster was located on the islands of Narragansett Bay and the other on the mainland. Connecticut's population, like Massachusetts, was distributed among three nodes, one on the east centered on New London and Norwich, one on the Connecticut Valley around the three original river towns (Hartford, Windsor, and Wethersfield), and a third in the west along Long Island Sound, dominated by New Haven. By the time of the Revolution the population of Connecticut and Rhode Island had expanded so that no areas in those colonies remained unsettled, although the density varied greatly between the older and newer towns. Only in Maine, Vermont, New Hampshire, and western Massachusetts were there appreciable amounts of unsettled land. Among the trends revealed by the data in the table is the impact of war on growth rates. The decades of King William's War, Queen Anne's War, King George's War, and the French and Indian War saw little or no population increase; yet during peacetime, growth accelerated. New Hampshire, as its erratic growth percentages demonstrate, was an exception to many population trends affecting the region.

3. In 1650, however, Virginia surpassed it, remaining the most populous for the rest of the colonial era.

Table I. Estimated Populations of Colonial New England
Numbers and Percentages of Increase

	1630	1640	1650	1660	1670	1680	1690
All New England	2,300	13,700	22,300	33,000	52,000	68,000	87,000
		550%	64%	50%	53%	30%	28%
Massachusetts	1,000	9,000	14,000	20,000	30,000	40,000	50,000
		800%	55%	42%	50%	33%	25%
Plymouth	400	1,000	1,500	2,000	5,000	6,000	7,000
		150%	50%	33%	150%	20%	16%
Connecticut		1,500	4,000	8,000	13,000	17,000	22,000
			166%	100%	62%	30%	29%
Rhode Island		300	800	1,500	2,000	3,000	4,000
			166%	87%	33%	50%	33%
New Hampshire	500	1,000	1,000	1,500	2,000	2,000	4,000
		100%	0	50%	33%	0	100%
Maine	400	900	1,000	*			

* Included in Massachusetts

   In spite of New England's population growth in absolute numbers during the colonial era, a consistently declining *growth rate* caused the regional share of total colonial population to decrease. In 1640, when the Great Migration of Puritans to New England ceased, New Englanders accounted for more than 60 per cent of the English population in North America. By the end of the seventeenth century that percentage had dropped to less than 40. By 1780, when the region's population is estimated to have been more than 600,000, the regional share of total colonial population had dropped to 25 per cent. The Middle and Southern colonies, on the other hand, experience higher growth rates, the result of both natural increase and immigration. In contrast, growth in New England was primarily the result of natural increase, for immigration to the region virtually ceased to be an important factor after the middle of the seventeenth century. Only in the decade following the Peace of Utrecht (1713), when the pressures pent up by long wars during the reigns of King William III and Queen Anne were released, did New England's growth outdistance its rival regions or surpass the colonial average.

   Limited immigration from abroad after mid-seventeenth century helped to preserve the "Englishness" of the New England population. Before 1700 the only non-English groups were Jews, French Huguenots,

1700	1710	1720	1730	1740	1750	1760	1770	1780
93,000	115,000	171,000	217,000	289,000	358,000	449,000	539,000	617,000
6%	23%	48%	26%	33%	23%	25%	20%	14%
56,000	62,000	91,000	114,000	152,000	188,000	223,000	235,000	269,000
12%	10%	46%	26%	33%	23%	18%	5%	15%
*								
26,000	39,000	59,000	75,000	89,000	111,000	142,000	184,000	207,000
18%	50%	51%	27%	18%	24%	27%	32%	12%
6,000	8,000	12,000	17,000	25,000	33,000	45,000	58,000	53,000
50%	33%	50%	41%	47%	32%	36%	28%	—%
5,000	6,000	9,000	11,000	23,000	28,000	39,000	62,000	88,000
25%	20%	50%	22%	109%	21%	39%	58%	41%

Source: Modified from *Historical Statistics of the United States*, U.S. Government Printing Office, Washington, D.C., 1960.

and blacks. The Jewish community lived chiefly in Newport throughout the colonial era; blacks and Huguenots primarily in the region's commercial centers. During the seventeenth century the black population of New England numbered less than a thousand; censuses taken shortly before the Revolution reveal that their total had risen to nearly 17,000— still the smallest total for any seaboard region in spite of the dramatic increase after 1700.[4] The federal census of 1790 was the first comprehensive document on which estimates of the seaboard's ethnic proportions may be based. Local records compiled before 1790 might be used to ascertain the ethnic characteristics of small areas, but such documents are inadequate for generalizations about large regions. On the basis of the nationalities indicated by the surnames of the heads of families listed in the federal census, it has been estimated that nearly 84 per cent of the

4. One interesting and somewhat inexplicable feature of the distribution of blacks in New England before the Revolution is that Connecticut, with more than 6000 blacks, had the largest number in the region. This is somewhat of an anomaly, for normally one would expect the largest concentration to be closely associated with the most active and largest commercial centers—Massachusetts or Rhode Island. But blacks in New England were principally household help, not field hands, and the probability that a larger percentage of Connecticut's population was rich enough to afford domestic servants than was the case for either of the other two colonies remains to be investigated.

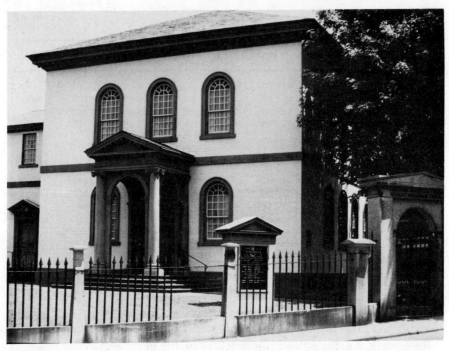

The Touro Synagogue in Newport, Rhode Island was an expression in the landscape of an unusual ethnic feature of that colonial urban center—the presence of a large, wealthy Jewish community. Built in mid-eighteenth century, the building has a plain and almost severe exterior, which belies its unique carved wooden interior. (*John H. Steenstra*)

total white population of the colonies was of English descent. In New England, however, that figure was approximately ten per cent higher, bearing out W. S. Rossiter's (former chief clerk of the Bureau of the Census) claim that "New England was almost as English as old England." Connecticut and Rhode Island with populations 96 per cent or more English were the highest, followed by Massachusetts and Vermont with 95 per cent or more, New Hampshire with 94 per cent, and Maine with 93 per cent. In the latter two colonies as elsewhere in eighteenth-century New England, Scots and Scotch–Irish accounted for the most numerous non-English elements, but they were less than 5 per cent of the population. The lack of ethnic diversity was to be an important factor in the development of insular Yankee communities in rural New England during the nineteenth century.

Population growth in the seaboard colonies has generally been considered beneficial because it spurred economic growth and encouraged the spread of people into undeveloped areas. Yet in a society like colonial New England, where most people depend on agriculture for their livelihood, population growth may create adverse relationships between man and the land—too many people on too little land with productive capacities. So it was, and noticeably so, in parts of New England by mid-eighteenth century. By that time, population growth in New England had caused a series of crises marked by land shortages and lowering economic output, particularly in rural areas. The agrarian portion of the economy offered little opportunity for above subsistence-level employment; both newly opened frontier farms and those in older sections operated at near subsistence. Since the period was one of limited urban growth, non-agricultural activities such as commerce or manufacturing failed to expand sufficiently to become alternative means of employment for a surplus population. In contrast to the other colonial regions, where expanding economic opportunities accompanied population increase, New England was a place where colonists could usually obtain the necessities of life but few of its luxuries.

Throughout the colonial period, increased densities in the older settlements were a direct result of natural population increase. Recent demographic studies indicate that most of New England's people were relatively immobile during the first century and a half of settlement. Until the mid-eighteenth century, land pressures were usually the consequence of depletion of preferred land types rather than an absolute lack of land, and demand for land was accommodated by divisions of remaining common land or the subdivision of family holdings. It has already been noted that these practices eventually led to the creation of new towns from the areas of the original towns. Thus in the older settled areas most towns found themselves with diminished acreages on which to sustain an increasing population. Through that process of town subdivision, depletion of unalloted lands, and increasing population, land values increased so much that by early eighteenth century most rural New Englanders could not afford to buy a self-sufficient farm. The options for rural families or men beginning their families were to go to the frontier (where land was cheaper but encumbered by liabilities) to await inheritance of parental property, or simply to seek better lands in another region.

The most desirable types of land were among those first parceled out. Later divisions involved less desirable lands—often marginal for cultivation because of thin, rocky soils—and New Englanders unable or unwilling to emigrate were left with diminished holdings consisting chiefly of such poor terrain. It was not surprising, then, that by mid-eighteenth century the quality of life in New England's older agricultural towns had dropped considerably; while the first and second generations of colonists were able to obtain good land and enough of it, the third and later generations had barely enough to scrape by on.

Statistics for two Massachusetts towns, Andover and Dedham, give an indication of problems created by increased population and reduced farm size, which by mid-eighteenth century were general among southern New England towns of comparable age and economic characteristics. Both towns had been reduced in size by subdivision, although Andover, with a smaller original grant, had more successfully resisted the process. At the beginning of the century, fewer than 1000 persons lived in Andover; by mid-century the population had nearly doubled. In the provincial census of 1765 it listed 2462 residents, making it one of the largest rural towns in the province, and by 1776 its population had risen to almost 3000. Inevitably, land pressures began to increase as the town's population density rose—from 41 to 50 persons per square mile in the decade 1765–76. More revealing of the land pressures associated with population growth, however, was the density in 1765 of 106 persons per square mile of *improved* land, a figure that had increased by 1776. Dedham's situation was comparable: in the same period it experienced reduced town size, increased numbers of people, and higher population densities on improved land. Between 1700 and 1750 its population had more than doubled, rising from 750 to more than 1600, and by 1776 there were more than 2000 inhabitants. Yet the area of the town by 1736 was about one-third its original size. Farms averaged less than 100 acres—at least a one-third reduction in farm size since the beginning of the eighteenth century—and many of those acres could not be cropped or used for pasturage.

URBANISM

Almost from the beginning of English settlement urbanism was a vital part of New England's regional character. New England probably had a higher percentage of urbanized population than other colonial regions, but that generalization is based on town population statistics, which do not differentiate by occupation. In the majority of towns, *most* of the population was agricultural, and one can only estimate the number of persons employed either totally or partially in non-agricultural activities (such as trades or professions) and who should be counted as part of the region's urbanized population. Those towns, then, which had large urban centers must suffice as the guides to the level of urbanism in colonial New England, even though a good portion of their populations might have been involved in agricultural activities.

In a seminal study of colonial urbanization, historian Carl Bridenbaugh classifies five seaboard places as "major urban centers," two of them—Boston and Newport—in New England. He also designates fifteen places as "secondary urban centers," nine of them in New England: New Haven, Norwich, New London, Salem, Hartford, Middletown, Portsmouth, Marblehead, and Providence (see Table II). Bridenbaugh based his study on late colonial censuses rather than on the spatial distribution of urban activities. Those figures represented the total population in the provincial subdivisions of the time—the town in the examples of New England, and other units in the remaining colonies. In the case of Boston and Newport the provincial population figures may be accepted as indicative of the degree of urbanism because of the small areal extent of the towns and the high concentration of urban activities within a comparatively limited space. For the secondary centers, however, town figures are less precise indicators of the amount of urbanization because

Figure 3-6.
TOWN HIERARCHY

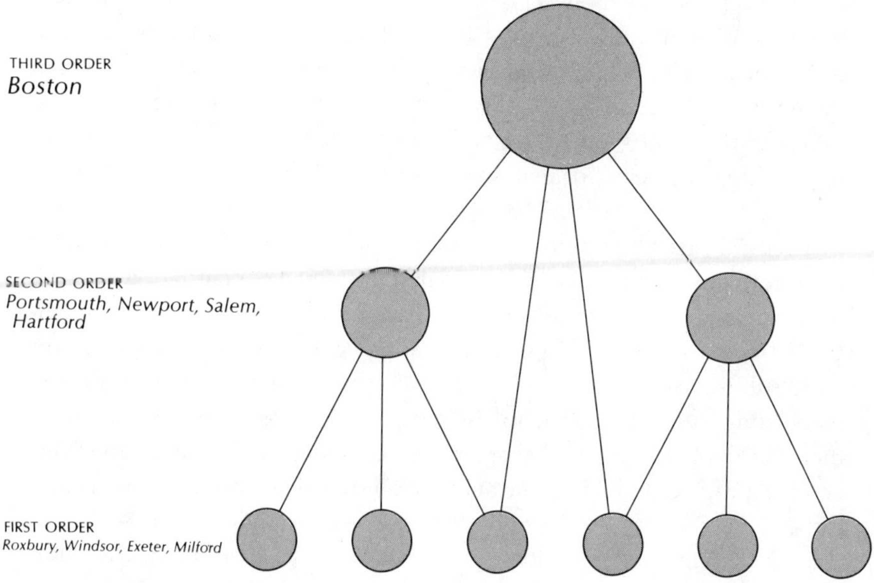

THIRD ORDER
Boston

SECOND ORDER
Portsmouth, Newport, Salem, Hartford

FIRST ORDER
Roxbury, Windsor, Exeter, Milford

Table II. Estimates of Populations of Urban Centers at Close of Colonial Era

---

(New England Centers are indicated by *)

1.	Philadelphia (1775)	40,000
2.	New York (1775)	25,000
3.	Boston (1775)	16,000 *
4.	Charlestown (1775)	12,000
5.	Newport (1775)	11,000 *
6.	New Haven (1771)	8,295 *
7.	Norwich (1774)	7,032 *
8.	Norfolk (1775)	6,250
9.	Baltimore (1775)	5,934
10.	New London (1774)	5,366 *
11.	Salem (1776)	5,337 *
12.	Lancaster (1776)	5,000
13.	Hartford (1774)	4,881*
14.	Middletown (1775)	4,680 *
15.	Portsmouth (1775)	4,590 *
16.	Marblehead (1776)	4,386 *
17.	Providence (1774)	4,361 *
18.	Albany (1776)	4,000
19.	Annapolis (1775)	3,700
20.	Savannah (1775)	3,200

Source: Carl Bridenbaugh, *Cities in Revolt.*

the area of the towns was larger; thus it may be assumed that those towns contained a lower proportion of the population directly engaged in urban activities—the remainder being agriculturists. In some cases, town records indicate the employment and activities of residents, so that differentiating between urban and non-urban portions of the populace is possible, but detailed analyses of such records are yet to be carried out.

A central-place hierarchy was inherent in the original town system, for in most towns the proprietors designated a site where central places were to be located (see Fig. 3-6). And expansion of the network was facilitated by the frequent dispersal of central-place services before towns were subdivided. Most town centers served as the seat of local government and provided leadership in religion, education, and trade. With the advent of the imperial wars in the late seventeenth and the eighteenth century, defense became another central-place service as stockades, forts, or garrison houses were built at convenient and accessible sites.

Some services or functions were not widely distributed. By mid-seventeenth century, counties were being created, and a selective hierarchy of political services began to develop. In the newer settled areas the functions of the shire village (county seat) were often shifted from village to village to reduce the time the townsmen spent traveling to and from court. But in older settled areas usually only one village was designated as the center of shire functions. Each colony eventually selected a center for its administration, when the practice of rotating the site of meeting for the colonial assembly was found to be inconvenient. New Haven and Plymouth, however, by virtue of their founding roles, were the undisputed political centers for their jurisdictions, and New Haven through its influential minister, John Davenport, tried to establish itself as a religious power as well. In the Bay Colony the pattern of shifting meetings of the General Court soon was abandoned, given the inconveniences of transporting men and records around the countryside. Instead the Court began meeting regularly in Boston, which as the largest center in the colony was best equipped to handle the sessions. Boston was also most frequently the home of the governor and other officials during the formative years; thus even when the Court was not in session the Bay Colony was actually ruled from Boston. The city's selection as the permanent capital made geographic sense and complemented its economic function as the primate center of the region. In New Hampshire, Portsmouth also served as both political and commercial center, but in Maine, because of the weakness of the proprietary government, a political focus failed to develop; further, such a focus was unneeded after the province was absorbed by Massachusetts. In Rhode Island a democratic and independent spirit kept the meetings of its assembly shifting among the major villages until a capitol building was finally erected in Newport early in the eighteenth century. The effective administration of the colony, however, was usually found in the home village of the governor.

Economic activities were prominent in the development of the spatial hierarchy of towns. Overseas trade, warehousing, and wholesaling were concentrated in a few coastal centers. Most specialized consumer services and manufacturers were found only in the larger centers, such as Boston, Salem, and Newport. And as the regional economy shifted from household to specialized handicraft production, artisans—glaziers, glovemakers, specialized metal workers, and bakers—began to concentrate in the larger centers. The designation of certain villages as market sites or fair sites in the tradition of old England enabled such places to establish commercial hegemony over the surrounding areas.

The villages in which political, economic, and professional activities were centered were functionally urban places, in some instances from the time of their founding. Yet to call the urban centers of colonial New England—small indeed by present-day standards—"cities" is misleading. In order to emphasize their contemporary conditions, they are here called *urban villages,* a term that differentiates them as unique functional places but still implies small size, an integral relationship with the town, and the presence of agriculture.

As the urban villages of New England prospered, population increased, the range of personal wealth expanded, specialization of labor became more common and new functions and services made their appearance. Consequently there developed demands for space which eventually produced distinct, segregated land-use zones in these villages (see Fig. 3-7). In most of the coastal urban villages, the core of urban functions was the site of overseas trade, the area in which wharves, warehouses, and merchant countinghouses were concentrated. Nearby but also occupying a site suitable for docking, were located ancillary services, including shipyards for repair and building of new vessels, sail lofts, and blacksmith's forges. Although ropewalks were essential to ship outfitting, they were usually found on the fringes of the built-up area because they required an acre or more and could not afford to locate along the congested waterfront. Commercial activities were usually located in the original town center or immediately adjacent to it, as in Boston

Figure 3-7.

MODEL OF FUNCTIONAL ZONATION IN URBAN VILLAGES

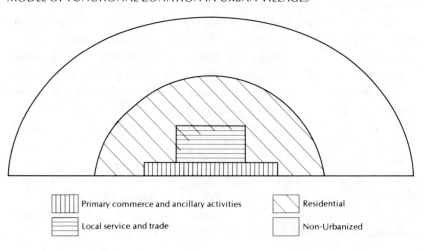

|||||| Primary commerce and ancillary activities   Residential

Local service and trade   Non-Urbanized

Market sites were an important part of colonial life. By mid-eighteenth century, New England's two largest urban villages had markets under cover—Faneuil Hall in Boston and the Brick Market in Newport. Daily commerce occupied the ground floor, while the upper story was an assembly or meeting hall. The small but well-proportioned Georgian style Brick Market of Newport is shown here, now surrounded by a modern shopping mall. (*John H. Steenstra*)

around Town Cove, or in Salem along South River. Some towns whose economic expansion was tied to overseas trade had original centers lacking adequate docking facilities. To accommodate the new activity a port site with deepwater anchorage and space for landside enterprises had to be selected—often some distance from the original town center. If the overseas trade flourished, the new site, as in Norwich, Connecticut, became the economic focus of the town, while the older settlement node languished or disappeared.

Local service establishments were originally limited in number, but as population and wealth increased and tradesmen became more specialized, such establishments became more numerous and varied. By 1750, specialized shops and services in most urban villages were grouped together, apart from but close to the primary commercial zone and creating

RESIDENTIAL PATTERNS AND HOUSE TYPES
IN URBAN VILLAGES

a

b

c

a. The urban villages of colonial New England were compact, with narrow streets and closely spaced structures. This view in a restored part of colonial Newport is of single-family dwellings built in the simple, straight-lined Georgian style of the first half of the eighteenth century. (*John H. Steenstra*)
b. The house that Paul Revere lived in at the time of the Revolution was built about 1680 in a popular English style distinguished by an overhanging second story and small, diamond-shaped windowpanes. One of the few buildings in New England surviving from the 1600s, the Revere House was fortunate to escape fire, and later, demolition crews. (*The New York Public Library*)
c. Wealthy merchants in the 1700s built large, Georgian-style mansions with the features visible in the Hunter House of Newport, Rhode Island. This view of the house from the waterfront shows the austere, straight lines and the symmetrical fenestration of that style. Evidence of wealth may be seen in the decorations over the windows and doors and in the use of the gambrel roof. (*Douglas R. McManis*)

a small business district. Since it was not unusual for trades and crafts to be conducted on ground floors of residences, manufactural and residential zones were often intermixed. Residential areas were located close to the income-producing sections of the villages because most workers walked to work. Housing for most of the population consisted of small, closely spaced single-family frame dwellings. Today the remaining sections of colonial Newport give a relatively undisturbed view of such an arrangement. Richer folk could afford to live in residential areas of lower density; their dwellings, which often were placed on higher elevations or

Figure 3-8. Captain John Bonner's Map of

overlooking the harbor, as at Newport, were located at a greater distance from the commercial areas but close enough to permit supervision of commercial activities. Beyond the residential areas were the fields, pastures, and garden plots.

Boston was not the oldest of the Bay Colony settlements, but it rapidly became the primary central place and largest urban village of New England. Boston surpassed its neighbors and competitors for many reasons; perhaps the foremost factor was that its government officials and clergymen lent the town from the day of its founding a prominence no other community enjoyed. Other residents—the scions of London mercantile families or persons otherwise connected with the English commercial world—quickly provided the know-how, capital, and connections that

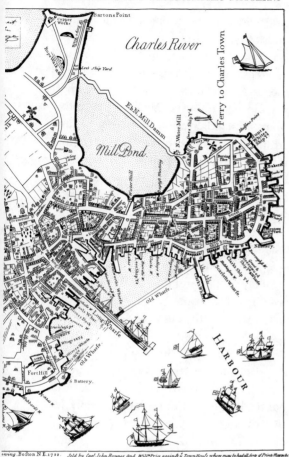

Boston, 1722. (*Massachusetts Historical Society*)

made Boston the leading trading center and entrepôt for colonial New England.

The urban functions of Boston were concentrated around Town Cove at the foot of three glacial hills that rose from the Shawmut Peninsula (see Fig. 3-8). There, wharves and docks were built. As the village thrived, the early paths became narrow, irregular streets. The concentration of leading merchants along Cornhill Street (a major thoroughfare named after the important commercial street in London) and its branches to the wharves was the first functional zone to emerge in the village. By 1650, wharves and docks had spread north across Mill Creek, and the shore of the North End was soon lined with shipyards and attendant activities. A dam was built to separate Mill Cove from the

Charles River, and Mill Creek was widened and deepened to accommodate two tidally powered gristmills. As a result of man-made changes to the creek, the North End became an island connected to the original peninsula by two bridges. Public areas and structures—the market, burying ground, churches, townhouse, and statehouse—were located a short distance inland from the wharves. Beyond the urbanized section were a few pastures and garden plots, but croplands were in short supply, and Boston was eventually granted non-contiguous tracts—Braintree and Muddy River (Brookline)—for farms. Even with the extra land, however, the village had to depend on foodstuffs from neighboring towns as well as overseas imports. By mid-seventeenth century, Boston's importance and influence were greater than its size indicated. Perceptive observers of the time called it the "regional metropolis," an appropriate description of its role as the primate urban center of New England. It is estimated that in 1650 there was a population of 2000 to 3000, accounting for roughly one-fifth of the Bay Colony's total—and that by the end of the century, the numbers had increased to some 7000.

Boston's degree of primacy was to wane in the eighteenth century, but no other urban village in the region developed such a broad base of activities or range of influence. Between it and the local service-oriented town centers there slowly emerged an intermediate category of urban villages. Often such centers were the shire towns, and in the case of Hartford and Portsmouth, the political centers of the colony as well. But more importantly the intermediate category villages were commercial centers. Springfield, Massachusetts, for example, became the retail-wholesale distribution center for the middle Connecticut Valley. Along the coast, places such as Portsmouth, Newport, New London, and Salem were the foci of a small but consistent overseas commerce, which was a small-scale model of Boston's. The consistency of that commerce distinguished these villages from smaller coastal ports such as Ipswich or New Haven, where ships only occasionally engaged in overseas trade.

The status of New England as the most urbanized section of the colonial seaboard until the mid-eighteenth century was symbolized by the primacy of Boston. The village's estimated population of 7000 in the year 1700 grew during the next three decades by 2000 persons per decade, but the largest increase occurred between 1730 and 1739, when its population increased by 4000. In 1740, which marked the apex of colonial Boston's growth, it had an estimated 17,000 residents, although by 1750, war and a smallpox epidemic had lowered the population to fewer than 16,000. Thereafter, Boston's population stabilized between 15,000 and 16,000. During the early years of the Revolution, Boston, like other urban centers occupied by British troops, suffered rapid depopulation. By 1776 there were fewer than 3000 inhabitants left in the village, but after the withdrawal of British troops its citizens began to return, and by 1780 the population had risen to 10,000—a figure, however, that was still well below the highpoint of the colonial era.

During the first four decades of the eighteenth century, Boston's population continued to increase. But after a decade of population loss (1740–50), a loss suffered by no other urban center—even in New England—and a stabilizing of population—also unique to Boston—the village had lost its position as the largest urban center in the colonies. By 1760, Philadelphia was the largest center, with almost 30,000 residents; New York, second with 21,000; and Boston, a poor third, with a stagnant population of only 15,000.

Newport (Rhode Island), the second largest urban center in New England at the end of the colonial era, had grown primarily as the result of expanding commercial activities after 1713, although it had been involved in the slave trade as early as 1696. Its pattern of continuous increase of population until the Revolution was more typical of colonial urbanism than Boston's growth pattern. In the provincial census of 1774, Newport had a population of slightly more than 9000, making it more than twice the size of its nearest colonial rival, Providence. But destruction of trade and capital during the Revolution had far more impact on Newport than on urban commercial centers elsewhere in New England, and Newport did not revive after the war as did other urban villages. Not until 1850 did the town again reach or surpass its population of 1774.

Like Newport, the other nine towns classified by Bridenbaugh as secondary urban centers belong to the intermediate order of the regional central-place hierarchy. These urbanized towns shared certain characteristics: each was founded and developed in the seventeenth century, each had a coastal location or direct access to the ocean, and each participated in overseas trade, the major growth component for centers in that order of the hierarchy. In the eighteenth century, when agriculture was stagnant and offered little opportunity for economic growth, few of the newer inland centers were able to duplicate the achievements of the older coastal centers. Only a small number of the former, which served mainly agricultural areas, were able to perform anything but localized town services, a fact which kept them in the lowest order of the regional urban hierarchy. However, some of the recently founded inland centers, such as Rutland, Vermont, showed indications of an enlarged range of services—stores, for example, which attracted buyers and sellers from other towns. But the development of enough activities to raise an inland town center to a higher order in the hierarchy was a phenomenon of the nineteenth century.

During the seventeenth century, Boston's near monopoly of overseas trade commerce was the critical factor in its rise to regional primacy, but during the eighteenth century, its dominance in that area was successfully challenged by the smaller second-order centers. They began to participate directly in overseas commerce, no longer depending on Boston as an entrepôt. They successfully copied the entrepreneurship that had been responsible for the center's rise to commercial power, and more than likely it was their commercial strength that held Boston in a static position during the second half of the eighteenth century. The trade of these smaller rivals, however, never equaled Boston's and, although its regional status had been considerably reduced, Boston remained the principal urban center in New England.

Suggested References

Bridenbaugh, Carl. *Cities in Revolt* (New York: Capricorn Books, 1964).
———. *Cities in the Wilderness* (New York: Alfred A. Knopf, 1955).
Carroll, Peter N. *Puritanism and the Wilderness* (New York: Columbia University Press, 1969).
Clark, Charles E. *The Eastern Frontier: The Settlement of Northern New England 1610–1763* (New York: Alfred A. Knopf, 1970).
Glass, D. V., and Eversley, D. E. C. (eds.). *Population in History* (Chicago: Aldine Publishing Co., 1965).
Greene, Evarts B., and Harrington, Virginia D. *American Population Before the Federal Census of 1790* (Gloucester, Mass.: Peter Smith, 1966).
Greene, Lorenzo J. *The Negro in Colonial New England 1620–1776* (New York: Columbia University Press, 1942).
Greven, Philip J., Jr. *Four Generations: Population, Land, and Family Life in Colonial Andover, Massachusetts* (Ithaca, N.Y.: Cornell University Press, 1970).

Haller, William H., Jr. *The Puritan Frontier: Town Planting in New England Colonial Development 1630–1660* (New York: Columbia University Press, 1951).

Leach, Douglas E. *The Northern Colonial Frontier 1607–1763* (New York: Holt, Rinehart and Winston, 1966).

Lockridge, Kenneth A. "The Population of Dedham, Massachusetts, 1636–1736" (*Economic History Review*, 2nd Series, XIX (1966), 318–44).

Mathews, Lois K. *The Expansion of New England* (Boston: Houghton Mifflin, 1909).

Mood, Fulmer. "Studies in the History of American Settled Areas and Frontier Lines: Settled Areas and Frontier Lines, 1625–1790" (*Agricultural History*, XXVI (Jan. 1952), 16–34).

Phillips, James D. *Salem in the Eighteenth Century* (Boston: Houghton Mifflin, 1937).

Powell, Sumner C. *Puritan Village: The Formation of a New England Town* (Middletown, Conn.: Wesleyan University Press, 1963).

Reps, John W. *Town Planning in Frontier America* (Princeton, N.J.: Princeton University Press, 1969).

Rutman, Darrett B. *Winthrop's Boston* (Chapel Hill, N.C.: University of North Carolina Press, 1965).

Sutherland, Stella H. *Population Distribution in Colonial America* (New York: AMS Press, 1966).

Warden, G. B. *Boston 1689–1776* (Boston: Little, Brown, 1970).

Whitehill, Walter M. *Boston: A Topographical History* (Cambridge, Mass.: Harvard University Press, 1959).

Whitney, Herbert A. "Estimating Precensus Populations: A Method Suggested and Applied to the Towns of Rhode Island and Plymouth Colonies in 1689" (*Annals* of the Association of American Geographers, LV (March 1965), 179–89).

Vaughan, Alden T. *New England Frontier: Puritan and Indians 1620–1675* (Boston: Little, Brown, 1965).

4 AGRICULTURE, FISHING, AND COMMERCE

The economic activities practiced in New England by the settlers were among the primary processes which transformed the indigenous landscape into one in various stages of Europeanization by the end of the colonial era. The first permanent settlers were aliens in a new habitat, faced with choosing sites for their pastures, croplands, farmsteads, and villages and with selecting materials for buildings and implements, for animal fodder, and even for foodstuff and dyes. At first, decisions about resource use were based on trial and error—the colonists had only their European practices and techniques to fall back on, and the European methods did not always work. With the passage of time, however, they accumulated a greater knowledge of the region's resources, and eventually a distinctive, "New England" way of doing things evolved. By 1720 the typical New Englander was native-born, with a century of American experience behind him to make decisions about resource use or site selection.

The same patterns of cultural change were equally true of other seaboard regions, and during the process of change the geographic effects had two profiles. The first was linear, or horizontal, associated with the expansion of settlement and spread of Europeanization into new areas, a sequence which may easily be mapped (see Fig. 3-1). The second profile is vertical, exhibiting changes in a single place over time after initial settlement. These vertical changes are variable in their impact—even on places that are close together. By the end of the colonial period the landscape of New England was a mosaic composed of many areal variations, the result of differential rates of change within the region. For example, the importance of historian Charles Grant's study of the town of Kent, Connecticut, is that it demonstrates local variation from the broad regional generalizations that other historians had defined for New England. The problem, then, in dealing with the vertical profile of change is to achieve a level of generalization which does not totally obscure local variations.

Economist Walt Rostow's model of economic growth is one in which the changing economic patterns of colonial New England as well as other seaboard regions may be cast. His model is designed to emphasize historical development by delimiting five sequential stages of economic growth. These are the traditional society, the preconditions for take-off, the take-off, the drive to maturity, and the age of high mass-consumption. Of these five stages only the first two apply to the period covered by this book, for New England was still in the preconditions for take-off for some years after Independence. In applying the model to New England it is assumed that gross regional patterns will dominate but not totally exclude local variations and that regional data need not coincide with the factual bases used by Rostow, for it is his model of temporal change, not his economic doctrine or national examples which are adopted here. If one views New England solely within the political framework of the United States, the region is reflective of the model's sequential aspects, for the region did progress from an agricultural society to an advanced industrial one. Yet it can not be ignored that during its first century and a half of existence New England was politically colonial—a collection of competitive colonies subjected to varying degrees of regulation from the mother country. Two important factors necessary to understanding the progression of the region through the early stages of the model are the consequences of that colonial status: (1) initial expenditure of manpower, capital, and resources was necessary to reestablish the traditional society of the colonists in a new environment and (2) interference from the mother country often had a critical influence on the economic activities of the colonies.

The basic features of the traditional society stage were introduced into New England in the decades immediately preceding the end of that stage in England. Few innovations marked its introduction—adoption of selected Indian foods and methods of cultivation and the use of raw materials unknown in England. In the Rostow model the preconditions for take-off stage is a broad transition period from the pre-Newtonian world to one geared toward industrialization. In New England, however, that stage was characterized by more subtle and gradual change extending over a longer period of time than in Britain.

From the viewpoint of cultural geography, the entire colonial period in New England was an era of transition from an indigenous landscape into one dominated by urbanization and industry by mid-nineteenth century. In Rostow's terminology, once the transplanted traditional society had established itself and more and more colonists abandoned agriculture for non-agricultural activities such as land speculation, war profiteering, manufacture, and commerce, the transitional stage—pre-conditions for take-off—had begun. Since that transition occurred at different times throughout New England it is difficult to give a precise date for its beginning. But certainly in southern New England the process was at work during the late seventeenth century and throughout the eighteenth. Fluid capital and managerial expertise were slowly accumlated and applied first to commerce and manufacture, then later to industry in the early nineteenth century. The value of the Rostow scheme thus is threefold: it permits generalization about a diverse region; it stresses the importance of colonial developments as antecedents of later national characteristics; and it provides a comparative basis for other seaboard regions as well as other countries.

Agriculture

Throughout the colonial period New England easily fitted Rostow's definition of an agricultural society—75 per cent or more of its labor force was involved in farming. Except in urban centers, where trade, fishing, and central-place functions were the primary activities, or in coastal New Hampshire and Maine, where men seasonally alternated between fishing and lumbering, New England's towns were predominately agricultural. By the beginning of the eighteenth century, however, agriculture in New England had ceased to be an avenue to economic advancement, and the transition from the traditional society (even though most of the population remained closely tied to its colonial practices) to pre-conditions for take-off became more marked.

Early explorers had planted experimental gardens in New England to test soil fertility and the suitability of the land for English crops, but the Pilgrims were the first Englishmen to till the soils and to depend on its produce for subsistence. Their initial achievements, however, owed more to native than to English practices. After their first planting of wheat failed, they turned to the cultivation of maize by the Indian hill-and-hoe method, and turned livestock out to seek natural forage. The Pilgrims—like generations of pioneers after them—used such methods until the actual clearing of fields permitted them to return to more traditional European crops and techniques of farming. Yet American farmers never totally abandoned maize, which remains today a mainstay of American agriculture, although it is primarily grown as animal fodder rather than foodstuff. Indeed, the adoption of maize into human and animal diets was one of the earliest examples of cultural change among the seaboard colonists.

A survey of estate inventories and wills shows that maize competed with wheat and other grains of European origin throughout colonial times. By the mid-1670s the grain was so widely grown in southern New England that the younger Winthrop, the first American member of the Royal Society, was asked to prepare a report on maize and its cultivation for his colleagues in London. He explained that furrows about six feet apart were plowed and crossed with another set of furrows. Seeds were planted at the intersections of the furrows. When weeds surpassed the maize in height, they were plowed under. Once that process was repeated, the plants were "hilled"; that is, soil was hoed around the base of each plant to support it in later growth. Where fish or the remains of fish curing were available, they were placed in the hills under the seeds according to Indian practice. Some colonists added bean and pumpkin seeds to the maize hills, and so continued the Indian method of multiple cropping. The cornstalks then doubled as beanpoles, and the support of soil provided by hilling became even more important. In his report Winthrop observed that rightly or wrongly, many colonists believed that a field had to be planted with corn before it would yield a satisfactory crop of wheat in later growing seasons; he also noted that field preparations for maize were suited to summer wheat as well. Such procedures, described slightly more than half a century after the first English farmers had tilled New England soils, were still followed in the nineteenth century.

For several decades after settlement, New England was a region of agricultural surplus (in spite of its later being stereotyped as a region of subsistence or less), a surplus that not only sustained an increasing population but also provided a primer for overseas trade. The earliest English settlements (Jamestown, Sagadahoc) had depended on imported food

As settlers moved inland away from the salt and freshwater marshes of the coast, the preferred land type became large, grass-covered riverine terraces whose alluvial soils were easily plowed. The Connecticut Valley contained the largest areas of this type of land in New England. The view here is of the middle portion of the valley, looking southeast near Deerfield, Massachusetts. (*Douglas R. McManis*)

supplies, but the first New Englanders had to produce food to survive, and so tried to locate their farms on lands well suited to their immediate needs. One observer remarked that New Haven's poor record in farming was the result of a town site selected primarily for its qualities as a trading center rather than for agriculture. It has already been noted that the Pilgrims chose a site previously cleared and farmed by the Indians. Later settlers also often located on former Indian village sites; in so doing they avoided the laborious task of clearing trees and were able to start planting as soon after settlement as weather permitted. As the colonists pushed into the interior they often chose as settlement sites alluvial terraces where native grasses rather than trees were the ground cover; this meant an initially fertile soil that could be easily plowed, as well as fodder for livestock. Unfortunately the colonists' agricultural methods only served to hasten depletion of the soils. Crop rotation was rarely used, and fertilizers were usually limited to the manure that collected on the fields after the harvest when livestock were allowed to graze on the stubble.

   In later years, shortages of preferred land types forced many colonists to move onto the less desirable lands usually associated with agriculture

Marginal agricultural lands prevailed over much of New England. When the preferred types of land were allocated both along the coast and inland, colonists had to settle on land barely suitable for crops but often satisfactory for pastures. Such land had steep slopes, rock outcrops, and stony, thin soils. (*Douglas R. McManis*)

in New England. Rock-strewn fields, stone outcrops, and soils of marginal fertility only added to the general agricultural problems already besetting the region.

The principal food crops introduced from Europe were wheat, rye, oats, barley, peas, and varieties of kitchen-garden crops. Wills and estate inventories indicate that wheat was either the most widely cultivated or the most highly valued cereal in the early part of the seventeenth century, but that the grain was losing its status by the last quarter of the century—in some towns an early sign of soil depletion, in others the beginnings of the ravages of wheat blast. Barley was used in the brewing of beer, a popular beverage then as now; oats were chiefly animal fodder. Rye was cultivated as early as 1636 by the Puritans, according to the senior Winthrop, and on the light sandy, gravelly soils along the coast gave better yields than other grains. Later, as wheat became more difficult to grow, it had to be imported from the Middle Colonies and the Chesapeake Bay region; rye flour was used far more frequently than one might expect among a population whose basic preference was for wheaten breads.

As the source of flour most esteemed by their culture, wheat was among the first grains the English settlers tried to grow. The Pilgrims' first attempts ended in failure, but the Puritans were more successful, harvesting a small crop in the first growing season after their arrival in Massachusetts. Both winter and spring varieties were planted, but the latter proved more reliable in New England's climate. Although the grain was grown in most towns in some quantity, it became a specialty in the middle Connecticut Valley towns; one historian even claimed that every farmer in the towns of Northampton, Hadley, and Hatfield raised wheat for sale. But as early as 1680, reduced yields due to soil depletion were discernible in those towns. The wheat crop in southern New England was also adversely affected by the appearance of the wheat blast, now recognized as fungous black stem-rust. It first appeared about 1660 in eastern Massachusetts, and then spread into parts of Connecticut, eventually affecting wheat crops throughout the region. Its appearance in an area was usually followed by a marked decrease in wheat planting and a corresponding rise in rye and maize production.

Before the blast destroyed many of New England's wheatfields, grain was a prime marketable commodity in the coastal towns—both in the local trade and as an item of overseas trade, especially in the West Indies. And in a money-deficit economy, grain was accepted as payment for town or provincial taxes, a certain indicator of the value placed on it. Wheat especially brought high prices, and so could bear the cost of shipping over long distances. For example, John Pynchon often dealt with wheat in his Springfield–Boston trade, sending as much as 1500 bushels by way of river and coastal boats in one year (1652). The acceptance of grain for taxes also ensured the movement of surplus from farm to coastal urban villages. When production declined, however, the pattern reversed itself and the urban villages had to import wheat from the Middle Colonies and the Chesapeake Bay region as demands increased.

In spite of the repeated mention of cropping in New England, the actual amount of land under cultivation must have been small in comparison to total farm holdings. Evidence on which this conclusion is based includes wills and estate inventories, town records and tax rates, farmers' diaries, and petitions to colonial legislatures. For example, in a study of Kent, Connecticut, on the largest farm of some 247 acres (timberland not included in figure) only 56 acres were cultivated, or on another farm of 107 acres only 20 were plowed; most land was in pasturage or left unimproved. It follows that only a small number of acres was devoted to wheat production, or indeed to any crop. Still, the amount of surplus grain produced in early New England was remarkable for a newly developed region with less than optimum physical conditions for farming. Periods of shortage did occur, however, and sometimes were severe: in July, 1646, a plague of caterpillars destroyed much of the wheat and barley crop around Boston, and in the following year a short harvest forced the General Court to forbid the grain's export from Massachusetts. Shortages were also caused by the outfitting of vessels for voyages, especially in small villages along the northern coast.

Kitchen-garden crops played a generally insignificant role in the region's exchange economy. Yet they were necessary to local diets, and on most house lots a plot was set aside for the kitchen garden, where for the most part vegetables brought from Europe—cabbage, turnips, carrots, parsnips, onions, and herbs—were grown. Fruit trees were another major introduction of European husbandry to New England. Apple, pear, plum, quince, and cherry trees flourished; peaches did less well. Apples, however, were the most common. By the end of the seventeenth century, large apple orchards could be found in all of the older towns, for cider had become one of the most widely consumed beverages in New England.

The Pilgrims were also responsible for introducing European domesticated animals to New England—the natives had no domesticated animals except pet dogs. English barnyard animals—pigs, chickens, and goats—appear to have been plentiful soon after the Pilgrims arrived, leading historian Darrett Rutman to speculate that such creatures might have been crowded onto the *Mayflower* along with its other passengers. In 1624 Edward Winslow brought the first cattle to Plymouth, and in 1626 the settlers at Cape Ann received twelve cows. As late as 1626, however, there is no evidence of horses or sheep.

It was the Puritan colonists who made English livestock a standard feature of the colonial agricultural landscape. They were better financed and better equipped than the colonists who came before them, and nowhere was that advantage better displayed than in the Bay Company's shipments of livestock to New England. The 1629 fleet to Salem brought cattle, mares, swine, and goats. Thereafter most ships bringing emigrants to Massachusetts carried livestock. Shipments of goats were especially numerous in the early years—they were hardy beasts less apt to die in transit, took less space on board ship than cattle, and often served as ships' dairies during the Atlantic crossing. In 1633 John Mason imported a herd of Danish cattle to his colony at the mouth of the Piscataqua River; two years later an inventory of his plantation listed 58 cattle, 92 sheep, 27 goats, 64 swine, and 22 horses. After his death Mason's agent drove what remained of the herds—some of the animals had been stolen by the settlers—to Boston, where they sold for a handsome price. This event was one of the first instances of what was to become an important feature of the colonial economy—droving of cattle from a frontier range to an urban market.

Livestock for the most part had to survive on natural forage. Along the coast, salt marshes were valued as pasturage and sources of hay, while in the interior, freshwater marshes had comparable esteem and function. Small stacks of hay drying on wooden platforms (to raise them above water level) were a common sight in most towns. The open ground-cover created by Indian burnings provided much forage for the beasts, but as settlement expanded and burning ceased, such forage began to disappear. Because the configuration of the coast was irregular, there were many small peninsulas and necks where livestock could be pastured with a minimum of care and danger. The colonists valued such areas because water confined the roaming animals on at least three sides, reducing the labor of fencing. Islands, too, were valued for the same reasons.

Fields had to be fenced to protect crops from animals. At first wooden fences were erected, later low stone walls. Each town passed regulations governing the building and repairing of common fences, while other rules stated the responsibility of owners of destructive animals to owners of damaged property. With livestock roaming freely or under minimum control, frontiersmen, not only in colonial New England but for centuries later on the western frontier, faced the choice of penning their animals or fencing their crops. As long as livestock were expected to survive on forage rather than on supplemental feeding, farmers chose the former course, enclosing their fields instead of the beasts—a relatively simple procedure, especially in towns where fence-building was a communal task. Although many community aspects of colonial New England began to break down in the eighteenth century, a good number of farmers continued to enclose their crops, and the custom lingered on until well into the nineteenth century. The practice of enclosing animals generally became mandatory when a settlement had expanded to the point where no unimproved land was left for animals to forage. By that time, fences around fields served more to delimit fields than to protect crops.

The original hope that the native grasses of North America would provide forage comparable to the grasses of England proved false. While native American grasses appeared luxuriant, as animal fodder they were coarse, rank, and non-nutritious. Dried, they were even less palatable than fresh. Unfortunately, the colonists left England before the practice of preparing sown pastures with improved nutritious grasses became a part of English agriculture, and for decades most New England farmers simply allowed their livestock to survive on the poor grasses. Sowing of English grasses began sometime after the Puritan arrival, but it is impossible to determine the extent of their planting. In 1663 an Englishman writing of his travels in New England noted that clover thrived on coastal farms. Significantly, red clover had been introduced to the British Isles in 1633 and must have spread to the colonies only shortly thereafter. In 1665 an official report from the colony of Rhode Island mentioned the presence of "English grass." From such scant evidence one may conclude that imported grasses were present in the older coastal towns, but of course, not their abundance.

Cattle, both because of their value and their general vulnerability, received more supervision than other livestock. The cow-keeper, or herdsman, one of the few town employees, gathered the animals from their owners each morning, took them to pasture, and returned them in the evening. Usually a pasture on the unimproved lands of the town was used, but as previously mentioned, cattle were allowed to graze inside the fenced fields after harvest; and the manure they left served as fertilizer for the next growing season. In some towns the herdsman worked only in the spring, summer, and fall months, since the farmers kept their small individual herds on the house lots during the winter. But as cattle became more numerous, the pattern of livestock-care changed. Herds were divided into milk-producers and dry animals; the former kept under the watch of a town herdsman on pastures near the house lots, the dry animals sent to unimproved lands some two to fifteen miles from the farms. There they roamed freely and unattended until they were rounded up to be branded, marketed, or transferred to the milking herd. Brands, which were listed in town records to prevent duplication, were necessary to identify ownership. Thus began the so-called "cattle kingdom" (much of it, indeed, open range), which over the years migrated westward across the continent to the Great Plains in advance of cultivation.

At first the colonists followed the English custom of providing little winter shelter for their animals. They did not realize how poorly the animals fared in the rigorous winters, and further, they lacked labor to build barns. Only the hardiest beasts survived the process of natural selection that followed. From it, however, emerged a tough, often scrawny, but durable animal that could still produce milk, meat, and hides. It also served as a draft animal. With the division of cows into milk- and dry-stock herds, small one-story barns were built on house lots to shelter the milkers in winter, during which time they were fed cornhusks, cornstalks, and marsh-grass hay to supplement the meager remaining natural forage of the town plot.

Cattle were also an important marketable commodity—one that presented few transportation problems: the animals could walk to market. In the early years of Puritan settlement around Massachusetts Bay, the Plymouth colonists supplied the newcomers with cattle, the sales representing the only important economic stimulus to the Old Colony since its founding. That outlet and profit, however, lasted only about a decade, by which time the Puritan towns were producing surplus cattle of their own. By 1650, large herds from Lynn, Watertown, and Roxbury were being marketed in Boston. Elsewhere, animals were driven from the Connecticut Valley and Rhode Island to Boston, New London, and other ports, where they were slaughtered and packed for overseas shipment, principally to the West Indies. By the eighteenth century, droving from towns on the lower Connecticut to New London, Connecticut's chief port, was a standard operation. One of the first areas of specialized animal husbandry to develop in New England was located in Rhode Island west of Narragansett Bay. Because by New England standards the size of farms was unusually large—some were a thousand or more acres—the area was called the "Narragansett Planters," an attempt to liken it to the plantations of the southern colonies. The area's specialty was the breeding of riding horses called Narragansett Pacers, which were exported chiefly to the West Indies and Surinam, where the horses were favorites among the rich.

Other livestock found in New England included goats, swine, and sheep. The reasons for the popularity of goats have already been mentioned. But as more cattle were shipped to New England and bred there, the demand for and the number of goats declined. According to Edward Johnson, one of the first settlers of Massachusetts, "Goates which were in great esteeme at their first coming, are now almost quite banished. . . ."

Swine were both the most durable and troublesome of the imported livestock. They could forage where other animals could not and would defend themselves against dogs, wolves, and huntsmen. But they could also destroy fences and root out crops. To protect property, town regulations soon required that any free-roaming swine be ringed or yoked to stop their rooting or that they be kept some distance from fields. Swine were an important source of meat for the colonists—hence their tolerance in spite of the destruction—who brought with them from England preservation techniques of smoking, salt rubbing, and brining. By 1660, pork-packing had become a major commercial activity. Sometimes hogs were fattened locally for slaughter, the meat packed and sent to a port; others were driven to distant markets for slaughter and packing and shipment overseas. Although tax lists and estate inventories imply that a very small percentage of a farmer's livestock was swine, they were undoubtedly more numerous than such records suggest—their free-roaming habits made ownership and numbers difficult to ascertain.

Sheep were introduced to New England sometime in the second decade of English settlement. As late as 1627 apparently there were none at Plymouth, but as noted previously, Mason had a flock at the mouth of the Piscataqua before 1633. The transfer of these animals into the New World environment was not so successful initially as it was for other kinds of English livestock. Far more vulnerable than cattle or goats, sheep were constantly being attacked by untrained dogs and wolves. Bounties on wolf pelts were early established, but the problem was ultimately brought under control as settlement destroyed the wolves' natural habitat. Thus, by the end of the seventeenth century, wolves were pretty much a frontier problem, long since gone from the older settled towns, and the size of local flocks increased accordingly.

Sheep were valued primarily for their wool, secondly for meat. The importance of wool is indicated, according to Rutman, by the official encouragement of sheep-raising in Plymouth Colony during the depression of the 1640s. By mid-seventeenth century other colonies, faced with inadequate supplies of wool, repeatedly passed legislation to encourage the raising of sheep. Among the measures taken were restrictions on export, prohibition of slaughter, and exemption of flocks from town or provincial taxation.

As long as each owner was responsible for his own sheep, the number he kept was restricted to the few animals that his busy family could care for. Eventually, town flocks were formed under the supervision of town shepherds, who were constantly on the move from one unimproved pasture to another. These animals could deplete a pasture quickly and thoroughly; under such circumstances, of course, it was senseless to build stationary folds. Yet the flocks had to be protected at night, so shepherds were forced to put up, in each new field, crude shelters, or pens. In the middle Connecticut Valley towns, this problem was handled by the use of movable pens.

Rhode Island was the center of New England sheep-raising, supplying stock to other colonies; for example, when John Pynchon wanted to enlarge his flocks in the Connecticut Valley, he bought from Rhode Island dealers. Reports to London in 1665 and 1676 stated that Rhode Island had the most sheep in the New England colonies, a status that was maintained into the eighteenth century. The offshore islands of Nantucket and Martha's Vineyard, where moderate winters were balanced by the need to import forage, were also noted for sheep raising. Efforts to increase the productivity of the flocks by importing rams from England were frustrated by the British, who quickly tried to put a stop to such exports. But small-scale smuggling of the breeders into southern New England did occur, a little-known episode of colonial rejection of British laws a decade or more before the more publicized events immediately before the Revolution.

Horses, first brought to the Bay Colony from England, were augmented by a shipment of mares and stallions from Holland in 1635. They were suitable for both riding and draft power, although the colonists usually preferred oxen for draft animals. Horsemeat was not used as food, and only those able to afford riding animals owned horses. Like cattle, horses were to become an important export commodity in the West Indian trade, and as early as 1648 the animals were shipped to the Antilles from Boston. Indeed, throughout the eighteenth century, export of horses from southern New England remained a basic characteristic of the region's trade with the Indies. Much of that trade, of course, centered on Rhode Island and the Narragansett Pacers. The development of these fine saddle horses ranks with that of the Conestoga draft-horses in Pennsylvania among the major innovations in animal husbandry in the

American colonies during the eighteenth century. Associated with horse raising was the breeding of mules. In the pre-Revolutionary era, Windham County, Connecticut, and Worcester County, Massachusetts, were pre-eminent. Based on these examples husbandry appeared to be a more satisfactory solution to agrarian problems in southern New England than cropping.

The English settlers were soon able to turn parts of New England into a land that amply rewarded their labor, partially fulfilling the predictions of early promoters. At mid-seventeenth century, a year after the elder Winthrop's death, Edward Johnson summarized the transformation that had taken place in the nearly three decades of English permanent residence in New England:

> The Lord hath been pleased to turn all the wigwams, huts, and hovels the English dwelt in at their first coming, into orderly, fair, and well-built houses, well furnished many of them, together with Orchards filled with goodly fruit trees, and gardens with variety of flowers; There are supposed to be in the Mattachusets Government at this day, neer a thousand acres of land planted for Orchards and Gardens besides their fields are filled with garden fruit, there being, as is supposed in this Colony, about fifteen thousand acres in tillage, and of cattel about twelve thousand neat, and about three thousand sheep.

A century later the promise and optimism found in the statements of Winthrop and Johnson proved ill-founded, for the general farming that the colonists wished to practice was feasible only for one or two generations. Thus, instead of becoming prolific, New England's agriculture fell into bad times, except where specializations such as animal husbandry in the Narragansett country or flax-seed production in southwestern Connecticut enabled farmers to withstand the regional trend. It was basically a matter of mediocre soils compounded by poor methods and by farmers unwilling to change their ways. More and more farmers switched from tillage to grazing, especially in the older towns of southeastern New England. Cattle required less time and effort than did crops, and in more remote areas they provided a solution to the problem of accessibility to market. But the trend toward animal husbandry as opposed to cropping was also observable where market opportunities in neighboring urban centers were already established, so that one is tempted to project a trend to a dominant pastoralism throughout New England in the decades before the Revolution.

Appeals to colonial assemblies for relief from provincial taxes were often accompanied by statistics to illustrate the deteriorating nature of the petitioning town's economy, although one recent historian, Charles B. Grant, casts doubts on the veracity of many of the petitions. Of one from Kent in northwestern Connecticut Grant concluded: "Thus the petition fiasco ended. Kent proprietors got nothing, and if local evidence is trustworthy, they deserved nothing." Grant, nevertheless, supports the basic thesis of many petitions—that increasing population pressure on available lands was a major factor in New England's eighteenth-century agrarian decline. Two other Connecticut towns petitioning for relief from provincial taxes about 1780 claimed to have only four or less acres of tilled land per family. That figure is in line with Grant's conclusions on the amount of land needed for subsistence in the town of Kent—a family could not subsist on such small acreage unless it had other sources of income for food and other necessities; he summarizes that an average of 14 acres of plowed land plus an average of 75 acres of other types of land was the minimum in late colonial or early national times for a family to live above subsistence levels.[1]

There were similar claims from towns in eastern Massachusetts, and wills and estate inventories further document the general reduction of cultivated lands in New England. If the pleas of the petitioners were valid, then the shift from general farming to animal husbandry had not solved the basic agricultural problem for most of New England. Nevertheless, returns from agricultural labor continued to provide most farmers of the region the necessities, if not the luxuries, of life.

Thus farmers began to abandon the cultivation of crops, particularly in the older settled areas, because of generally decreasing production. Indeed, by the early eighteenth century, local urban centers began to depend, as did Boston, on imports of wheat from the Middle Colonies and the Chesapeake Bay region. Some observers familiar with the British Agricultural Revolution attempted to place the blame for New England's failing agricultural system solely on the farmers, calling special attention to their outmoded farming techniques, such as infrequent crop rotation

1. James Lemon's recent study of southeastern Pennsylvania provides a challenging contrast to Grant's conclusion. Generally the physical conditions for agriculture were better in southeastern Pennsylvania than in New England, so that one might expect fewer acres were needed to meet subsistence requirements. Yet Lemon concludes that a family needed 26 to 35 acres of plowed land to rise above subsistence level. The differences in subsistence requirements which each researcher estimated are worth further study because each describes his study group as economic "maximizers"—persons who seek more than a subsistence livelihood.

and random use of fertilizers, and their steadfast resistance to the adoption of new plant species from Europe. The anonymous author of *American Husbandry* (1775), generally accepting the philosophy and practices of Arthur Young (the founder of the British Agricultural Revolution), devotes an entire chapter to the problem: "Errors in the Rural Management of New England." He presents the usual arguments of the British agrarian reformers. But he also recognizes that New England's agricultural plight resulted not only from inefficient farming methods but also from physical conditions, noting that while the decline in wheat acreage was brought on by poor farming methods, it was certainly exacerbated by the blast. In general, however, he agreed with the earlier criticism of Jared Eliot (Connecticut author of *Essays Upon Field-Husbandry in New England*, the first book on agricultural practices to be written in the colonies) that the failure of the colonists to accept and to use new farming methods was the principal cause of the region's problem. This failure, which was evident throughout the colonies, but especially in New England, is one instance of "delayed innovation," a factor unaccounted for in Rostow's scheme of economic progression.

Given the limited inherent potential of New England's soils, it is questionable whether the new British intensive methods of field maintenance would have been economically viable in New England. A small minority, most prominent among them the above-mentioned Jared Eliot, argued for the adoption of the British methods as the solution to the region's agricultural problems. In his book, Eliot proposed a broad system of crop rotation combining both familiar and newly introduced crops and the use of fertilizers such as manure and lime, in addition to advising on methods of reclamation. Few New England farmers, however, followed such suggestions for improvement. To them the options by middle and late eighteenth century seemed to be (1) stay on the farms and make the best of the deteriorating situation, (2) turn to some profitable form of agricultural specialization, (3) migrate to better lands outside the region, or (4) abandon agriculture altogether and take up urban employment.

So the agricultural landscape of New England slowly changed into one dominated by pastures and orchards. Maize and rye were the major crops, oats and barley the minor ones. By the time of the Revolution, wheat had practically disappeared from the fields of the older settled areas and it was grown chiefly on the newly opened soils of the frontier. There it flourished free from the ravages of the blast until once again poor management depleted the soils of nutrients and weakened the crop's ability to resist disease. The general regional trend, however, was reversed in some areas where specialty crops foreshadowed later types of successful intensive cultivation: onions at Wethersfield, Connecticut, tobacco at several places in the Connecticut Valley, and flax seed in Fairfield County, Connecticut, for export to Ireland were grown successfully and profitably by the closing decades of the colonial era. During the same period, cattle husbandry both for butterfat and beef emerged as the principal agricultural activity in southern Vermont, western Massachusetts, and northwestern Connecticut. The Narragansett Region continued to emphasize livestock for export.

Fishing

Fishing did not employ so many men as did agriculture, but its importance to the regional economy cannot be stated simply in terms of employment. The potential of New England's fisheries was early advanced as an argument to stimulate English interest in the region. Explorers in the early seventeenth century observed abundant fish in the coastal waters; after those explorations English promotional literature depicted New England's fisheries as the equal—if not superior—to those of Newfoundland. It is surprising, then, that the realization of the potential came so late after the recognition. Fishing vessels from England's West Country invariably returned home laden with fish. Even before permanent settlement began in 1620, the promoters' aims had been achieved: the quest for fish had brought many Englishmen to the shores of New England. But the camps they set up along the coast and on offshore islands such as Richmond and Monhegan were only temporary; these men set sail for English ports as soon as they had collected a cargo. Such freelancing was threatened by a monopoly in fishing granted to the Council for New England as part of its original prerogative. But the freelancers simply ignored the monopoly, and the Council found itself unable to enforce its privilege, a victim of rising opposition to Crown-granted monopolies in Stuart England and an impossible policing problem in its vast, poorly delimited domain. The monopoly was finally dissolved in 1634 (with the surrender of the Council's patent), having made almost no impression at all on the transatlantic fishing pattern.

While English-based use of New England's fisheries predated permanent settlement, efforts to establish New England-based operations were not immediately successful. The Pilgrims had planned to use fishing as one means to repay their debts to the Weston group and other creditors, but their efforts failed, while English ships returned laden with fish from New England waters. Still later the Dorchester Company's station at Cape Ann failed to become a profitable operation. There are probably several reasons for the Pilgrims' lack of success: they were not fishermen in the first place; their equipment was inferior to that of the English; and their success in the fur trade and the later market for agricultural commodities (which the arrival of the Puritans opened) encouraged the non-seafaring folk of Plymouth to seek their fortunes on land, not sea. The failure of the Dorchester colony at Cape Ann is more complex, for in theory it had the necessary elements to make the station flourish. Yet the repeated influx of skilled men and equipment failed to do so, and that fate is all the more inexplicable when one considers that in later colonial times, other ports along the North Shore of Massachusetts Bay such as Gloucester and Marblehead became the leading fishing ports of the region.

The rise of commercially operated fisheries in New England stemmed from the change in economic relationships between the colonies and England in the 1640s. With the advent of the English Civil War in that decade, West Country fishermen no longer visited the region's fishing banks, and New Englanders, apparently at first motivated by a search for winter employment, slowly began to take their place. They started with the most meager of equipment, but fish and labor were both plentiful, and soon the colonial fishing enterprise ranked as a basic economic activity in New England, its success perhaps first measured by Winthrop's estimate of 300,000 cod caught in 1641. Small fishing villages began to spring up along the coast, particularly north of the Piscataqua, and on offshore islands. In contrast to the earlier stations, which catered to the transient fishermen from England, the new stations were permanent settlements. It was soon learned that the earlier promotional claim that New England had two fishing seasons (Newfoundland had but one) was true, so that in many a coastal town the farmers went to sea in the winter to harvest cod.

At first the colonial fishermen worked two major northwestern Atlantic fishing areas, both within the Gulf of Maine, which extends from Cape Cod to the southern tip of Nova Scotia (see Fig. 4-1). The first area consists of a series of small fishing grounds, or banks, generally within twelve to fifteen miles of the mainland coast, stretching from

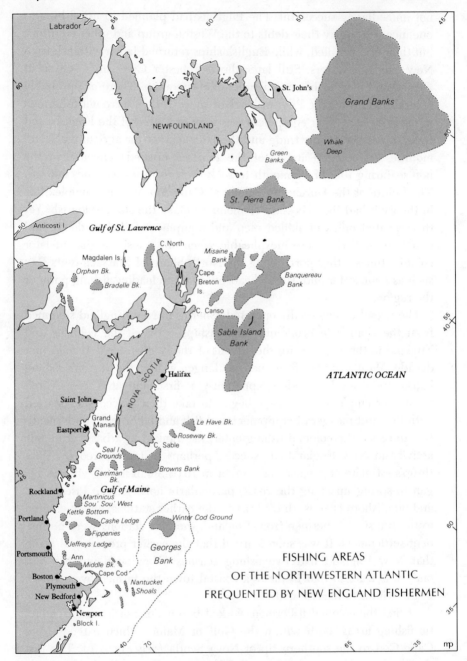

Figure 4-1.

Grand Manan Island southward to Stillwagen's Bank between Cape Cod and Cape Ann, with outlyers off Nantucket and Martha's Vineyard. These grounds abounded in cod, haddock, and hake.

Further into the Atlantic a second chain of large banks extend southwestward from the Grand Banks of Newfoundland. George's Bank, the largest fishing ground in the Gulf of Maine, lies directly east of Cape Cod and Nantucket. Continuing northeast are Brown's Bank and Seal Island Bank, while the Grand Manan, German, and Marblehead banks are smaller and lie somewhat closer to shore. These grounds, according to historian Raymond McFarland, were "unsurpassed for the abundance and variety of the catch of fish." Cod, hake, haddock, and mackerel were the principal catch.

By the 1660s, fishermen from New England were sailing to a third area of the northwestern Atlantic—the Newfoundland fisheries. They first fished the Sable Island Banks, some 200 miles off the Nova Scotian coast, and by the 1670s, when English participation in those fisheries was declining, New Englanders had successfully established themselves in the heart of the Newfoundland Banks. Between 1670 and 1675 more than 600 vessels from New England were employed there. But the extension of fishing into those northern waters brought the colonists into conflict with the French on sea as well as on land.

As fishing changed from an English to colonial operation, stations on the offshore islands lost their dominance, and mainland villages such as Kittery or Marblehead became New England's principal fishing ports and supply depots. The locations of the fishing grounds close to the home ports meant that processing of the catch could take place in port rather than on a distant, deserted beach, and wooden stages, on which the fresh fish were placed for processing, became an integral part of the waterfront in New England's fishing villages. But curing was still done elsewhere, for some fishermen continued to put ashore at any convenient, unoccupied beach to cure their catch. There they cut the firewood neces sary to the curing process; seawater was boiled down for salt to rub on the fish, and fires were kept going to provide smoke and heat for drying. The uncontrolled cutting of timber by those fishermen was probably a major factor in the depletion of Maine's coastal forests.

Even during the period of English dominance of the New England fisheries, they were included in Boston's commercial hinterland. In the mid-1630s, island stations off the coast of Maine started to ship dried cod to Boston's merchants, and by mid-seventeenth century, dried fish gathered from the expanding fishing operations of the region's seamen, had become the single most important item in the overseas commerce of New England. A mutually dependent relationship was forged between the fishermen and the urban merchants, who traded cod to southern Europe and the West Indies.

By the end of the seventeenth century, imperial conflicts had started to affect the New England fisheries. Expansion of the activity had ceased; indeed to enter certain grounds had become dangerous, and many former areas fished in peacetime were declared off-limits in war-time. The depredations of the French and their Indian allies had con-stricted settlements along the northern coast, particularly east of the Piscataqua. Many villages were abandoned, most of the ships left to rot, and the fishermen left to find other employment. South of the Piscataqua the impact of warfare was less, but nevertheless noticeable. Because dis-stant staging areas were unsafe and because the French molested ships at sea, sailings from ports in Massachusetts were restricted as well. A final tactic used by the French to destroy New England's fishing enter-prise was the glutting of markets, chiefly with fish from the Newfound-land fisheries, which forced a ruinous drop in the price of the now-restricted New England catch. The colonial fishermen thus had good reason to share the farmers' and merchants' antagonism for the French and their Indian allies. Each group desired political adjustments that would stop French interference with their economic activities.

The generally depressed state of fishing during the last quarter of the seventeenth century and first decade of the eighteenth was partially compensated by the rise of whaling. By 1690 whaling was becoming a major activity in ports along the southeastern coast of Massachusetts. Even the offshore islands were involved, for Nantucket, which was to be-come one of the world's great whaling ports in the nineteenth century, was then participating on a small scale. Increased demand in the colo-nies and western Europe for whale oil for household lighting and baleen, or whalebone, for the fashion industry seems to be the principal explana-tion for the emergence of this specialized activity and its later expansion.

The restoration of peace in 1713, following King William's and Queen Anne's wars, permitted a revival of the fishing economy. Settlements re-appeared along the Maine coast, and the schooner, a fore-and-aft rigged vessel well suited to both deep-sea and coastal fishing, was developed at Gloucester's shipyards. By the early 1720s, Canso (on the strait between Cape Breton Island and mainland Nova Scotia) had emerged as an important site in the fishing trade; there fishermen exchanged barrels of dried fish for cargoes brought in on merchant ships, many of them owned by New Englanders. Marblehead moved to the foreground as the leading fishing port of the colonies, followed closely by Gloucester, relative positions the two villages held until the Revolution. By 1731, the fishery was employing more than 5000 men annually and in that year sold 320,000 quintals (hundred-weight) of dried fish. Production continued to increase over the years, with cod accounting for more than half the annual catch. The renewed harassments of King George's War and the French and Indian War caused irregularities in fishing and production as the earlier imperial wars had done. But the treaty signed in 1763 finally freed the colonial fishermen of the molestations and annoyances of their French enemies. Thus in the decade preceding the Revolution, the fishery was restored to its role as a leading colonial employer and as the source of the most lucrative item of colonial commerce.

Commerce

Trading between New England and western Europe predated permanent settlement by many years. Yet during the process of early settlement, commerce was primarily one-way, from England to the colonies. Distribution of goods was handled by merchants, located for the most part in Boston, who originally may have ranked low in the hierarchy of the London mercantile community, but who nonetheless had acquired there the experience requisite of successful merchants. Of the initial Puritan settlements, Boston attracted an unusually high percentage of the migrants from the predominately Puritan-oriented London commercial class, who had both the skills and contacts needed for success in commerce. Boston quickly emerged as the most prominent of the Bay Colony towns, attracting the largest number of new immigrants to the region. The ships carrying new settlers also carried cargoes placed on board by enterprising merchants or by the ships' captains themselves for sale. Rather than sail back with empty holds, ships' officers sought return cargoes, which encouraged the movement of goods from the town's immediate hinterland. Thus, shortly after settlement, a distribution network soon extended throughout the settled portion of New England, with Boston as the region's entrepôt. Small coastal boats, and later, ox-drawn carts were the means of circulation.

The colonial exchange structure was deficit in money and specie, and, although values entered in ledgers often hid the fact, most bills were paid in produce or labor rather than cash—in essence, the region functioned as a bartering economy rather than as a cash-exchange economy. Townsmen bought needed items from local storekeepers with their agricultural surplus or a specified period of labor. The surplus thus accumulated at the town level was in turn transported to the urban villages, where wholesaling took place. Foodstuffs found a ready market there among the urbanites, who did little farming, and among the new immigrants, who, although they had not yet established themselves, were a source of new capital. Commodities such as grain and cattle were shipped abroad to settle foreign accounts and to produce new capital. Non-agricultural items, such as pipe staves, masts, naval stores, and dried fish, were the principal items of foreign trade.

The "hinterland" pattern of trade, with local surpluses moving to consuming-exporting centers, from which imported goods were dispersed among the hinterland towns, dominated the commerce of New England for the first few decades after Puritan settlement. By about 1660, however, merchants had become one of the most valuable human resources of the region and were responsible for a critical reorientation of the area's trade. Instead of sending English goods into the hinterland, collecting products in return, many New Englanders started their own firms. Thus utilizing skills and knowledge of business practices, connections to overseas markets, and capital which they had either brought with them from England or developed locally, New England merchants in increasing numbers began to establish their own companies for direct trade with England, Mediterranean areas, and the West Indies. Often the credit and commercial contacts for such independent ventures were supplied through personal or familial connections with the world-wide commercial network centered in London. Eventually the independent activities of the New Englanders took on a pattern which permitted the rubric "triangular trade" to identify it, although the trade actually involved a complex exchange of cargoes and bills of credit in which cod (New England's contribution) was the major element.

Yankee ships laden with cod, pipe staves, masts, naval stores, and wheat sailed to many West European and Mediterranean ports, where their cargoes were sold or exchanged for more valuable items. These in turn were often bartered in other ports before the ship loaded for the return trip. New England merchantmen also sailed the Caribbean, and early became dominant in the West Indies trade, providing livestock, fish, and processed meats to the food-deficit islands, where most of the arable land was devoted to sugar plantations. By 1677, New England's ships also dominated the inter-island trade, making exorbitant profits, if the number of complaints registered with officials in London and with island governors is any guide. Yet their importance to the economic life of the islands was dramatically demonstrated in 1688, when the island of Nevis faced famine because Yankee captains, fined for abuses and illegal activities, had refused to trade there.

New Englanders were involved in the transportation of slaves to the Indies as early as 1645, but it is difficult to determine when such inhuman traffic became a regular feature of New England commerce. Ships running to the Mediterranean or visiting the wine-producing islands of Madeira, the Azores, or the Canaries often included a trip south to the West African slave coast, where they picked up human cargoes to be sold to West Indian sugar plantations. Few slaves, however, were ever sent to New England, as the low numbers of blacks recorded in the late colonial censuses or town records indicate. During the seventeenth century no New England port appeared to specialize in the slave trade, but in the next century both Newport and Bristol, Rhode Island, were acknowledged centers in the traffic.

In return for slaves delivered to the Indies, the New Englanders at first carried away tobacco, cotton, sugar, and bills of exchange to be honored in England. Molasses, however, was to become the mainstay of the West Indian trade, and, by the end of the seventeenth century, distilleries to convert it into rum were found in every major port in New England. The rum, used as a barter item in the slave trade, soon became a local problem in the colonies. By 1661 the General Court of Massachusetts had declared that overproduction of rum was a menace to society. So widespread was its consumption in the colony that during periods of short supply tavern-keepers diluted beer with rum, until stopped by Court order. The importance of rum for external commerce was twofold, allowing New Englanders to gain control of Newfoundland trade and to trade directly with the West African slave coast. In its simplest form the "triangular trade" involved trading rum for slaves, who were shipped from Africa to the West Indies and exchanged for molasses, which was then sent to New England to be distilled into more rum to keep the cycle operating. But, although rum accounted for a large percentage of the cargo of any ship leaving New England, its trade usually involved an intricate series of exchanges in many ports before the slave coast of Africa was reached. Voyages of over two years on the "triangle" were not un-common.

The use of rum in the Newfoundland trade did not involve human cargoes. The expanding fishery at Newfoundland, an island with few farmers and physical conditions not conducive to agriculture, provided New England's merchants with a lucrative market for foodstuffs—a smaller model of the market they had originally held in the West Indies. Yet in the long run the sale of rum was to prove more valuable than trade in foodstuffs, especially when New England's exportable food surpluses declined. In England, competitors for the Newfoundland market argued that rum was the principal cause of debauchery there and attempted unsuccessfully to keep the New Englanders out of the trade; English hostility was also based on fears that Newfoundland, like New Hampshire and Maine, might fall under the political dominance of the Bay Colony, and on the claim that the New Englanders were smuggling French and Dutch goods in violation of English navigation acts—even during wartime.

The trade to southern Europe emphasized cod and pipe staves. Cod, because it was cheap, had a ready market in Protestant and Catholic countries alike. Pipe staves, used for wine casks, were an important trade item in Iberian ports and in the major wine-producing islands in the Atlantic—the Canaries, the Azores, and Madeira. The wine received in trade was one of the few items New Englanders could sell in England. Unlike the West Indies or the southern mainland colonies, New England failed during the colonial period to achieve a direct mercantilistic relationship with the mother country. With the exception of masts, the region produced no commodity that was not obtainable elsewhere or produced in Britain. The Middle Colonies had much the same problem, but there, at least, grain had become a mainstay of inter-colonial trade.

The diffuse trading patterns developed by New Englanders during the seventeenth century continued to flourish with little variation in the century that followed. Boston's role as the dominant regional entrepôt declined relatively as merchants and ship owners in places like Newport, New London, Providence, or Portsmouth successfully challenged Boston's hegemony and established direct trading connections of their own. One consequence of that new commercial independence was that Boston's population remained fairly static during the eighteenth century, while the populations of the other urban centers continued to grow.

In an era when governments subscribed to mercantilist political-economic philosophy and legislation, commerce was one of the colonial activities most subject to imperial controls. Especially in the eighteenth century the British government passed acts aimed at curtailing colonial trade and raising tax money. As long as such acts were not too rigorously enforced, the colonists learned to adjust—usually by circumventing the acts legally or extra-legally, especially where enforcement officers were absent. The situation changed after 1763, however, when the British government, freed of the long-term contest with France for primacy in North America, not only passed new regulatory acts but also started to enforce old as well as new legislation. The new policy fell harder on the merchant community of New England than it did on those of other colonial regions. Thus conflicts between New Englanders in violation of the parliamentary acts and royal enforcement authorities were among the most bitter controversies between Crown and colonial subjects in the decade before the American Revolution.

Suggested References

Bailyn, Bernard. *The New England Merchants in the Seventeenth Century* (Cambridge, Mass.: Harvard University Press, 1955).

Bidwell, Percy W., and Falconer, John I. *History of Agriculture in the Northern United States 1620–1860* (Washington, D.C.: Carnegie Institution, 1925).

Bruchey, Stuart. *The Roots of American Economic Growth 1607–1861* (New York: Harper and Row, 1968).

Bruchey, Stuart (ed.). *The Colonial Merchant: Sources and Readings* (New York: Harcourt, Brace & World, 1966).

Bushman, Richard L. *From Puritan to Yankee: Character and Social Order in Connecticut 1690–1765* (Cambridge, Mass.: Harvard University Press, 1967).

Eliot, Jared. *Essays Upon Field Husbandry in New England* (New York: Columbia University Press, 1934).

Grant, Charles S. *Democracy in the Connecticut Frontier Town of Kent* (New York: Columbia University Press, 1961).

Hedges, James B. *The Browns of Providence Plantations: Colonial Years* (Cambridge, Mass.: Harvard University Press, 1952).

Jameson, J. Franklin (ed.). *Johnson's Wonder-Working Providence, 1628–1651* (New York: Charles Scribner's Sons, 1910).

Judd, Sylvester. *History of Hadley* (Springfield, Mass.: H. R. Huntting & Co., 1905).

Lockridge, Kenneth A. *A New England Town, the First Hundred Years: Dedham, Massachusetts, 1636–1736* (New York: W. W. Norton, 1970).

Lounsbury, Ralph G. *The British Fishery at Newfoundland 1634–1763* (New Haven, Conn.: Yale University Press, 1934).

McFarland, Raymond. *A History of the New England Fisheries* (New York: D. Appleton and Company, 1911).

Morison, Samuel E. *The Maritime History of Massachusetts* (Boston: Houghton Mifflin, 1921).

Rostow, W. W. *The Stages of Economic Growth* (Cambridge: Cambridge University Press, 1960).

Rutman, Darrett B. "Governor Winthrop's Garden Crop: The Significance of Agriculture in the Early Commerce of Massachusetts Bay" (*William and Mary Quarterly*, 3rd Series, XX (July 1963), 396–415).

———. *Husbandmen of Plymouth* (Boston: Beacon Press, 1967).

Walcott, Robert R. "Husbandry in Colonial New England" (*New England Quarterly*, IX (June 1936), 218–52).

Winthrop, John Jr. "The Description, Culture, and Use of Maize" (*Philosophical Transactions* of the Royal Society of London, XI–XII (1676–78), No. 142, pp. 1065–69).

5 FORESTRY, SHIPBUILDING, MANUFACTURES, AND COMMUNICATIONS

Forestry

The forests of New England were among the most valuable resources in the new homeland. They contained familiar hardwood and softwood species as well as a few trees the colonists had never seen. The presence of familiar trees—oaks, elms, maples, and willows—spared the colonists the problem of immediately experimenting with unfamiliar species, such as walnut, chestnut, hickory, and varieties of conifers. The early settlers' needs for wood was basic: it provided fencing and lumber for their shelters. From it they fashioned their tools, their furniture, their dishes, and most other household utensils. It was their only fuel. Thus, in the selection of any settlement site, a local supply of wood was a primary consideration.

Yet wood was not always close at hand. The colonists preferred open clearings and the generally treeless riverine terraces because they were thought to be more defensible, and, of course, there was none of the laborious task of tree and stump removal in preparing fields for crops. Then, too, much of the woodland in southern New England, like much of the eastern seaboard and the Appalachian area, was most likely open and park-like, not a dense, continuous forest as tradition would have us believe. So the problem of a wood supply was present almost from the beginnings of settlement. Trees within hauling distance of a new settlement were rapidly cut; in fact, depletion of accessible timber was so quick that within a decade of settlement many of the first-established towns had imposed regulations to preserve remaining trees, while newly planted towns often included cutting regulations among their first legal acts. A local timber shortage was often the first ecological crisis to be visited upon a town; soil depletion came later. The regulations (which usually applied to timber remaining on common lands and not to timber on assigned property) restricted cutting to certain times of the year and to selected parcels only, banned the cutting of some species altogether, and prohibited commercial use of any of the cut wood. But the New Englanders, who later proved so adroit at circumventing legislation from London, ignored local regulations not to their liking from the start. Their most frequent stratagem was to poach timber from the tracts of absentee owners or from ungranted lands within or outside the town, a practice that remained familiar on the American frontier for decades.

The town sawmill was a community enterprise, built and maintained by the town for its residents. At first the colonists used huge handsaws: a cut log was placed over a large open pit on a cross timber, and two sawyers manned the saw, one standing in the pit and the other on the cross timber. Needless to say, it was a backbreaking task, and it is not surprising that sawmills were among the first public structures to be built in the early towns. It was expected that the town mill would primarily satisfy familial needs, but once the commercial value of planks, pipe staves, and other types of boards became known, cutting increased greatly and many a farmer spent part of his winter preparing boards and staves for sale or exchange in nearby towns or urban centers. Occasionally farmers sold to the merchants' agents, who during the summer travelled the countryside contracting with the farmers for their winter's labor. Farmers also cut logs for fuel-deficit urban centers and, if a forge or furnace was in the vicinity, wood for charcoal. During the eighteenth century two other types of forest use rose to prominence: the preparation of pot ashes and pearl ashes—from which lye for soap-making was leached—and maple-sugaring. Making of pot or pearl ashes was particularly common on the frontier, where trees and stumps were burned to clear fields, and provided a small income to numerous farmers. At first the colonists tapped sugar maples for their own use only (cane or beet sugar was not to be had), but later, imbued with the same spirit that marked many enterprises in New England, many of them started to make maple sugar commercially, and by the late 1700s a large portion of the production was earmarked for the markets of the urban villages. In some communities, maple orchards were planted to make collection of syrup more systematic and more convenient.

The settlement of each New England town brought problems concerning forest allocation. Individual families were assigned timbered acreage, but the question of ownership of timber on unallotted lands or in the commons was often left unanswered and in later years became the source of bitter, acrimonious disputes among the townmen—some of whom argued that the town proprietors were merely trying to keep a valuable resource under their control or for their own use. As farm consolidation replaced parcelling of non-contiguous plots, the task of guaranteed timbered lands to each family became more difficult. Planting trees on a portion of a consolidated holding or retaining an uncut plot on a farm was perhaps the origin of the farm woodlot, a feature so typical of farmsteads west of the Appalachians in the nineteenth century. Still, to save their own timber, which often was in short supply, many farmers in defiance of the numerous town regulations governing use of unallocated land, simply helped themselves to timber from the commons or from land owned by others.

In spite of efforts to preserve the local forests, New Englanders cut trees at an alarming rate. By the eighteenth century, efforts of towns to curtail cutting could no longer be viewed solely as efforts of the propertied class to monopolize a needed raw material for its exclusive use. A genuine ecological imbalance existed: most of New England's remaining timber was to be found far from the areas where it was most needed. Raw timber and cheap boards for housing could only be sent to areas of high demand where cheap water transport was available, as it was between Massachusetts Bay towns and coastal Maine.

Deforestation was most noticeable, of course, immediately around those villages with the highest population densities and in areas such as the lower Piscataqua, where the manufacture of forest products was emphasized. By the early 1700s the urban villages often depended almost exclusively on supplies brought in from the woodlots of less urbanized neighboring towns or from distant forest lands. A change of urban architectual style from wood to brick helped to reduce the demand for timber, but that reduction was minimal, for New Englanders never developed the taste for brick housing that characterized other seaboard colonial areas. Even in Boston, the largest and wealthiest of the region's urban villages, brick construction was limited to a few public structures—markets, meetinghouses (churches), and the capitol building. Occasionally a wealthy merchant built himself a brick mansion, but the preference for wooden houses was true of all classes in colonial New England and continued long past the Revolution. As a result, fires were endemic in the agglomerated settlements and the repeated destruction of buildings only served to exacerbate timber shortages.

Shipbuilding

The first English ship to be built in New England antedated permanent settlement by more than a decade: the *Victory*, which sailed to Virginia and made at least two Atlantic crossings, was built at the Popham Colony. Yet for all its later importance the shipbuilding industry had a rather slow start in New England. The Pilgrims built no ships until two decades after their arrival, and it was only in the context of changes effected by the more enterprising Puritans and their economic activities that shipbuilding began to emerge as a basic manufacture of the region.

The original impetus for shipbuilding came from the colonists' needs for transportation and communication. Water traffic along the often foggy New England coast was hazardous, but the colonists found it the most convenient way to maintain trade and to exchange news among their scattered settlements. Early examples of colonial-built coastal craft were the *Blessing*, a 20-ton vessel built on the Mystic in 1631 for John Winthrop, Sr., and another built at Boston in 1633. The construction of ocean-going vessels coincided with the depression following the Great Migration: as ship arrivals from England decreased, the colonists feared that they would become isolated. Their remedy was to build their own ocean-going ships, among the first a 300-ton vessel in Salem and a 150-ton vessel in Boston in the early 1640s. Even Plymouth joined the competition in a small way with the laying of the keel for a 40-ton bark.

As New England-based commerce developed and expanded, vessels owned and built by the colonists became the mainstay of the carrying trade. Further stimulating the expansion of shipbuilding in New England were the Navigation Acts, which restricted trade to English ships, and dislocations and destruction caused by the English Civil War.

Part of the expansion included the construction of ships for English owners; this in spite of frequent complaints that the timbers of New England ships rotted faster than those built in England or in the southern colonies. Apparently, however, such fault was not common among colonially owned ships; therefore one must conclude that either the New England shipbuilders were in the habit of providing inferior wood for the contracted ships or that the English owners found it as a matter of pride impossible to admit that a vessel constructed in New England was the equal of an English-made one. The commissioners of the Royal Navy not only refused to contract for colonially built ships but also consistently refused to purchase New England timber on the grounds of its higher price and lower quality. But the inferior reputation of the Yankee ships did not reduce their salability, and construction in colonial shipyards for the British merchant marine grew steadily in the eighteenth century.

Before the end of the seventeenth century, ships and boats were built at many places along the coast of New England. In some areas coastal and riparian timbers were soon exhausted, and the yards for building of small vessels moved inland, closer to the needed timber; in winter the completed vessels were sledded over the ice and snow (pulled by oxen) to a stream where they were launched after the spring thaw. The yards for larger vessels, however, remained on deep-draft sites, dependent on timber shipped in from uncut areas and on riggings and outfittings imported from England. Later, local manufacturers began to produce outfittings, and the large yards became the focus of a complex of shipbuilding trades. Nearby were located the ropewalks, smithies, canvas works, and other enterprises necessary to put a ship into final sailing form—an early example of manufactural linkage in New England.

The major areas of shipbuilding at the end of the seventeenth century were Massachusetts Bay with foci at Boston, North River, and Salem; the lower Piscataqua River; and the lower Merrimack River. A fourth major concentration was then emerging around the settlements of Narragansett Bay. Not surprisingly, because of its active maritime commerce, Boston by mid-seventeenth century was the leading center of New England shipbuilding, a role the town retained into the next century. The yards and contributing trades were concentrated in its North End. Satellite centers were across the Charles River at Charlestown and up the river at Cambridge. Salem, with secondary centers at Marblehead and Gloucester, was an early rival to Boston, and by the 1670s, Ipswich ranked as a major producer. On the lower Piscataqua River, Kittery, Exeter, Dover, and Portsmouth had many yards after mid-seventeenth century. At that time the activity had also extended up the coast to York and Saco in Maine. Newbury was the principal site of the yards on the lower Merrimack, but the pattern of many yards dotting the river's banks for some distance upstream resembled the distribution along the Piscataqua. In 1646 another major concentration of shipyards began southeast of Boston at North River, with Scituate as its center, and in the years 1674–

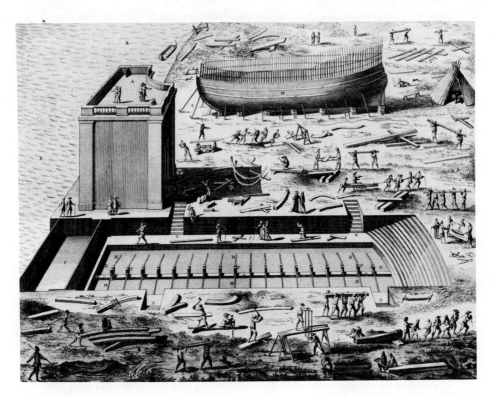

Shipbuilding required the skills of many different craftsmen. This composite sketch from Diderot's *Encyclopédie* (1747) shows the many crafts necessary to assemble a ship, such as laying the hull, and sawing and shaping timbers. Only the preparation of masts and riggings are omitted from the scene. (*Columbia University Libraries*)

96 it launched more ships of high tonnage than either Boston or Salem, its only rivals in scale of production. Vernon Briggs, a local nineteenth-century historian listed the building of fifty-four vessels in the North River area during the seventeenth century.

Small-scale operations were also numerous and widely distributed, particularly along the southern coast. On Massachusetts' southwest coast, ships were built at Bristol (then part of the Bay Colony), Rehoboth, Swansea, Taunton, and Freetown (now Fall River). In Rhode Island, ship construction began in 1646 at both Portsmouth and Newport; by late seventeenth century, Providence and Tiverton were also constructing small craft. New London, which after mid-seventeenth century became Connecticut's chief port, also was its principal shipbuilder. By

1660 it had a shipyard, but its output was mostly small vessels. Small craft were also built at Stonington and on the Mystic estuary. Between 1678 and 1699 many vessels, all less than 100 tons, were constructed and outfitted at the Connecticut towns of New Haven, Middletown, Milford, Lyme, Stratford, Haddon, Glastonbury, and Killingworth.

By the beginning of the eighteenth century, shipbuilding had emerged as one of the two largest non-agricultural industries in New England. In scale of operation, numbers of workers supported directly or in ancillary activities, volume of materials consumed, and volume of output, only the region's fishery stood as a rival. Demands for fishing vessels, for colonial and British merchantmen, and for occasional warships kept New England's shipyards and supporting processors busy for most of the eighteenth century except during brief periods of economic slump. The principal areas of shipyard concentration remained where they had developed during the previous century, as did the small yards.

Even before the end of the seventeenth century, the major colonial shipbuilders were experiencing difficulties in obtaining supplies of satisfactory ship timbers. The shortages were most acute in the Massachusetts and Narragansett bay areas, where deforestation had proceeded the most rapidly. Timbering in the Piscataqua area was not so intense, but by mid-eighteenth century the quality and quantity of supplies from the Piscataqua hinterland had also declined, as more and more land was cleared for agriculture. Shipbuilders had to go further and further afield for supplies—usually to the coast of Maine, where water transport for the logs or cut timber was available. In wartime, when the Maine supplies were curtailed, local softwoods were often substituted for the northern hardwoods. Much to the distress of ship owners and masters, the softwoods rotted more rapidly, making the ships more expensive to maintain and difficult to sail.

Unfortunately, only fragmentary figures indicating the volume of production from New England shipyards during the eighteenth century are available. Historian Bernard Bailyn's analysis of the records for the years 1697 to 1714 concludes that slightly more than one-fourth of the vessels registered in Massachusetts at the turn of the century—nearly thirty per cent of the total tonnage serving the province—had been built in Boston. Scituate was the second-ranking builder at the time, a statistic that validates Briggs's claim that the North River area was one of the major ship producers in the colonies. Salem and Charlestown were the only other centers that had contributed more than ten vessels. Other centers that

had built fewer than ten—were Cambridge, Ipswich, Newbury, Gloucester, Beverly, Lynn, Salisbury, Amesbury, Milton, Plymouth, Weymouth,
Hingham, Taunton, Swansea, and Bristol; of the province's important
coastal towns, note that only those of Cape Cod are omitted.[1]

Bailyn's figures show variations from year to year in the number of
vessels built in Massachusetts. But more importantly, from the geographic point of view, they show the gradual concentration of shipbuilding in Boston, both in number of vessels built and tonnage, while the
relative importance of Scituate, Salem, Charlestown, and Milton declined. In Milton, building of registered vessels virtually stopped from
1702 to 1714, although Gloucester enjoyed brief prominence as a major
secondary center during the same years. The number of Massachusetts-
registered vessels built in other colonies of New England during that period declined. While the records indicate the locations of the shipyards,
they give no indication of the total production of the non-Massachusetts
yards. The statistics available for the rest of the colonial era are sketchy,
but they suggest that throughout New England the basic locational patterns that had evolved by the early eighteenth century did not change
greatly.

THE MAST TRADE

One of the most valued trees of the New England forests from the Piscataqua northward was the white pine—unsurpassed for use as ships'
masts. It was strong and straight, and because of its unique length (as
much as 100 to 120 feet at maturity), shipwrights were able to fashion
strong, single-piece masts for even the largest ships of the time (masts
made from shorter European trees had to be pieced together). In recording a 1634 shipment of masts to England, Emmanuel Downing, a
prominent Puritan London merchant, suggested that legislation be en-
acted to permit shipment of white pine masts to England only. Nothing
was done at the time, but the suggestion foreshadowed later efforts to
institute restrictive cutting policy—eventually known as the "Broad Arrow"[2] policy. In 1653 the first shipment of masts to England for the Royal

1. Omission of the names of small settlements on Cape Cod from those registration
lists should not be interpreted to mean the absence of maritime activities. Many
Cape towns, such as Provincetown and Sandwich, supported a few fishing vessels
as well as small shipyards. But those activities were small scale and rarely directly
involved in inter-colonial or overseas trade; hence they usually escaped the notice
of officialdom and are absent from registry lists.
2. An act of 1729 designed to protect white pine authorized an arrow to be carved
into the bark on any tree reserved for the Crown. Only royal officials could touch
the trees so branded.

Navy took place, a trade which continued until the Revolutionary War. The Navy consistently found fault with New England ship timber, but colonial masts were always highly prized.

The mast trade was originally centered at Portsmouth, New Hampshire, and remained there until mid-eighteenth century. The cutting areas, however, slowly expanded up the Piscataqua River and its tributaries as well as into southern Maine. Felling the tall pines without breaking their trunks (their value, of course, was in their extraordinary length) required special skills. Trees suitable for masts were unevenly distributed throughout the forest, so that preliminary surveys were necessary to select areas in which the tallest pines were the most numerous. Selective cutting then had to be observed. Once a cutting area had been chosen, a roadway was opened to a stream. Smaller trees were cut around the "big stick," as the mast pine was popularly called, to break its fall so that it would not be broken or shattered. Samuel Sewall, the noted Massachusetts jurist and diarist, described the view of a mast being hauled to a nearby stream by seventy-two oxen as a "very notable sight." The logs were then floated individually downstream (with luck undamaged by rocks or falls during that journey) to the mast houses of Portsmouth, where they were hewed into masts.

The finished masts left Portsmouth in specially designed ships,[3] usually the product of New England shipyards. The cargo was considered so valuable that in wartime the slow-moving mast ships often had a naval escort to protect them from enemies. Besides England, where the Royal Navy was the largest single consumer, masts were sent to Portugal, Spain, Holland, the West Indies, and other seaboard colonies. The colonists attempted to keep the non-English trade going even when England was at war with the buyer, an additional source of friction was between Crown and colonial over mast policy. Affecting the supply of masts were, of course, the settlers; to them a Crown tree was no different than any other when they were clearing fields. Lumbermen too felled any and all trees for sawtimber—partly, it should be noted, in response to expanding shipbuilding. Until the late 1680s the English government did not interfere directly with mast collection or trade; after that time the Crown responded to the Navy's needs and reserved all mast trees under the "Broad Arrow" policy. Officials were appointed to supervise and en-

---

3. The unique feature of the mast ship was its single open hold in mid-ship, large enough to accommodate the tall masts. The long, open middle section seriously impaired the seaworthiness of the vessels, which were slow, cumbersome, and vulnerable to enemies as well as natural hazards.

force the Crown's forest regulations; thus, even before the end of the seventeenth century, the long and tortuous feud between colonists and home government over the exploitation of the forests of New Hampshire and Maine had begun.

In line with the general philosophy of mercantilism then expressing itself in selected legislation for the colonies, the British government attempted to control masting during the early decades of the eighteenth century. It tried to restrict cutting, to establish Crown ownership over trees of specified heights, and to curtail illegal exports. Those actions led to increased conflict between royal officials and the colonists who, although they continued to cut and export masts to established markets, were cutting the prized white pine to make shingles, clapboards, and barrel-staves, all items more profitable to them than masts. Shortly before the Revolutionary War, Governor John Wentworth of New Hampshire, hoping to end the repeated clashes between officials and poachers, proposed to reserve certain areas exclusively for the royal masts and to open other Crown lands to unrestricted cutting. The quarrel, of course, was ended in a different way.

By mid-eighteenth century, depletion of mast trees accessible to Portsmouth had been accomplished, and the center of mast collection moved to southern Maine. As early as 1720, regular shipments of masts were leaving Falmouth (now Portland) and its nearby rival, Scarborough. At mid-century not only had Maine become the leading mast producer of the northern colonies, but Falmouth had surpassed Portsmouth as the principal export center. In the summer of 1761 a massive forest fire started in New Hampshire and spread eastward to Casco Bay, destroying in its path the tracts on which both Portsmouth and Falmouth relied for their masts. In the aftermath of that fire, mast collection extended eastward along the coast of Maine and further into the interior, where streams were available for floating of the pines to the Falmouth mast houses. By the eve of the Revolutionary War both Bath and Machias were shipping masts, reflecting the eastward shift of mast collection.

Manufactures

Despite British mercantilist restrictions a great deal of manufacturing and processing arose in New England, some activities even privately receiving encouragement and capital from England. Primary processing of agricultural products necessary for day-to-day life (spinning, weaving, fulling, gristmilling, cheese- and butter-making, and the like) was ubiquitous. Of course, the colonists depended heavily on English manufactures and continued to depend on them well into the nineteenth century, long after political ties were severed; even so the variety and scale of manufacturing in New England advanced steadily.

Certain types of local service manufactures were quickly established in towns. Foremost among them was gristmilling, which produced the flour used in every household. Appropriate sites on streams with sufficient waterpower to run the mills were often some distance from the town center. Today the name Mill Street is usually a reminder of the path that once led from the house lots to the mills. In some instances a dam and pond had to be constructed in order to insure a constant flow of water to the mills, and like the street names many of those dams and ponds are still part of the southern New England landscape. However, in a few towns good stream sites were not available; there the colonists had to turn other sources of energy—in Boston, for example, windmills were erected—or they had to pay to have grain milled in neighboring towns. Needless to say, good millers were in great demand, and the towns were constantly bidding among themselves for their services; among the lures used to attract and keep a good miller in a town was the promise of land grants, freedom from town rates, and the promise of a large portion of the milling fees.

Other manufacturing enterprises that were also a common sight in colonial New England were sawmills, smithies, cobblers' shops, and tanneries. As in the case of the gristmills, if a town lacked one of those operations but thought it could support it, its leaders attempted to attract the needed craftsmen, using the same lures that had attracted the millers. Among the first enterprises to expand beyond the function of local service were tanneries—chiefly those in the region's principal seaports. In the seaports there were numerous demands for a variety of leather products. Hides for tanning were easily obtained from slaughterhouses.

Fabrics were one of the volume imports of New England, a major item in the chronic trade deficit between the region and England. Nevertheless, most households produced homespun for daily wear, and farmers and craftsmen often wore leather clothes. It has already been noted that some colonies took official measures to enlarge their flocks of sheep in order to increase the production of wool and colonially made woolen cloth. Yet fulling (a process of shrinking and thickening woolen cloth) remained a bottleneck in local production. The amount of fulling—a

LEATHER-MAKING

Swelling of hides was the first step in leather production. The hides were immersed in vats of lime water so that the pores expanded and hairs loosened. After the hides were sufficiently bloated, they were "beamed," or scraped with a sharp blade to remove the hair, fat, and other surplus flesh.

space-consuming process and one requiring a great deal of skill—that could be achieved in a household was limited, so that surplus wool production was restricted as long as a village had no mill. Fullers, of course, were in great demand, and many towns attempted to remedy the situation by licensing fulling mills, but few were actually built because of the shortage of fullers to operate them. So fulling mills often did not appear in a town until years after settlement. One was reported in Roxbury in 1655, some twenty years after the founding of the town; in Plymouth the first fulling mill was built in 1656; the mill in Waterbury, Connecticut, was opened only after a twenty-year interval, in 1676. However, during the last quarter of the seventeenth century the number of mills, particularly in the older towns, had increased, and by the century's end the production of domestic wool cloth had also increased. Even before mid-seventeenth century there were a few examples of more concentrated production. Rowley, Massachusetts, stood out in particular. It was settled in the late 1630s by a group of Yorkshire clothiers, who continued

A tanning yard in which tanning vats or pits were the principal equipment
was the center of the manufacture. In the vats, layers of hides were alternated with layers of tanning bark and submerged in water. Because the
tanning solution was strongest at the bottom of the vats, hides tended to tan
unevenly. Thus, several vats with solutions of varying strength were needed,
and hides were moved from one vat to another during the 12 to 18 months
they were in solution to insure uniform tanning. Three phases of the tanning
stage are shown here: On the left the first pit is being prepared with the
layers of bark and hides; in the second pit the tanning action is in progress;
workers at the third pit are either removing the finished hides or moving
them to a different vat. Colonial tanning was more primitive than as shown
in these etchings from Diderot's *Encyclopédie*, but the methods were the
same. (*Columbia University Libraries*)

their Old World trade in the New, erecting a fulling mill by 1643. The
trade flourished and by 1660 Samuel Maverick, one of the earliest settlers, could note that the wool cloth producers of Rowley "drive a pretty
trade, making Cloath and Ruggs of Cotton Wool, and also Sheeps wooll."
The trade continued successfully for several decades.

Early efforts to produce iron in New England illustrate the problems
of manufactural developments in a mercantilist colonial economy, where
the high cost of labor and chronic shortage of money made a return on
investment difficult even when both a satisfactory resource base and
widespread demand coexisted. The second attempt to produce iron in
the colonies (the first attempt was in Virginia, but before the works

could be completed, they were destroyed in the Indian uprising of 1622) had its start when the younger John Winthrop returned to London to obtain capital for equipment and trained laborers; there he found backers who were more than willing to invest in colonial iron manufacture. Pig iron importation would not only benefit the mother country but would earn them a handsome profit as well. For several decades English ironmasters had found it more and more difficult (and expensive) to meet demands for iron as public and private consumption increased. As the Royal Navy grew, it required not only more iron but more wood as well. Wood was the ironmasters' chief problem—needed to produce charcoal for use in the iron furnaces, it was also in demand for many other civilian and military purposes. In England, deforestation was affecting the traditional areas of iron production, so much so that the English were already importing iron from Europe—especially from lands around the Baltic Sea, where timber for charcoal was plentiful and competition limited. That of course meant a continuous outflow of English bullion into foreign coffers. Small wonder that the proposal to produce and import iron from an English colony found willing investors, in spite of the limited information Winthrop was able to give them about the realities of starting up such an operation in a wilderness. One difference of opinion appeared when the General Court of Massachusetts approved Winthrop's scheme; it specified that no iron was to be shipped from the colony until local needs had been met.

Late in 1643 Winthrop returned to the Bay Colony with workers and equipment. He planned to use ores from bogs near the coast, and so undertook a reconnaissance of the bogs between Cape Elizabeth, Maine, and Marshfield in Plymouth. Why he did not make such a survey before he sought funds is unknown, but one may conjecture that he was familiar enough with the bogs around Massachusetts Bay to have some idea of their potential before he left for England. Because the surrounding forests were still relatively uncut, Winthrop's chief locational problem in determining the site was the presence of bog ores in sufficient quantity to run a furnace. He considered the bogs around Braintree to contain the best quality ores—good enough, evidently, to justify the large expenditures which he had to make to buy the necessary land, which was in private hands by that time. Winthrop's spending, considered extravagant by the London backers, led to his dismissal. But his successor set up the Braintree works, which remained active until 1653 when lack of water due to a drought stopped production.

Bog ore mining. This etching from Diderot's *Encyclopédie* is a European version of marine mining—or bog ore mining as the practice was called in New England. Reflecting the artistic fashion of the time, the background has been filled in with a walled village and hilly landscape suggestive of the style of Claude Lorrain. (*Columbia University Libraries*)

In spite of Winthrop's preference for the Braintree site, the main center of the fledgling manufacture was to be at a site in Saugus (then part of Lynn), where a forge and a furnace were built about 1645 on the mouth of a small stream where it entered Massachusetts Bay. Few documents about that operation survive, but it is known that the furnace used ores scooped from nearby bogs, charcoal from timber supplied by local farmers, and flux brought by boat from Nahant. Eventually the Saugus works reached a maximum capacity of eight to ten tons per week—enough to satisfy many of the Bay Colony's needs and even to provide a small surplus for at least one shipment of pig iron to England. But the level of production was not consistent, and the London sponsors complained of no profits. Indeed, surviving ledgers of the company suggest that much of its sales were in barter—exchange of iron pots, for example, for wood or labor rather than cash; thus, while the operation was undoubtedly of great importance to the local economy, it could neither produce a marketable surplus for England or acquire enough cash to satisfy investors. A monopoly on production of iron within the Bay Colony, tax exemptions, and other privileges extended by the Massachusetts General Court were not enough to keep the Saugus works operating, particularly since its managers were often inept, and the furnace closed down sometime in the 1670s. The legacy of the Saugus works is reflected in the words of one early New England historian, William Hubbard, who wrote: "Instead of drawing out bars of iron for the country's use, there was hammered out nothing but contention and lawsuits which was a bad return for the undertakers."

In 1653 the Leonard brothers set up a furnace at Taunton and a forge at Raynham, then in Plymouth Colony. Bog ore and timber came from the towns' common lands; water from a pond created by a dam on Two Mile River. Production reached twenty to thirty tons annually. The operation, which continued for decades, was a financial success, even paying dividends now and then. Iron bars from the operation occasionally served as a medium of exchange throughout the neighborhood, and the area remained a major producer of iron throughout the colonial era. The Leonard family exemplifies what may have been the crucial element for successful iron manufacture in colonial New England—an element so often lacking—good management. Many successful operations in southern New England involved the Leonards, and their talents even spread beyond the region, members of the family associating with iron production in New Jersey and New York before the end of the colonial period.

In the meantime the younger Winthrop had moved to New London, Connecticut. Still interested in producing iron, he visited the New Haven colony in the spring of 1655 to determine if the bog ores in the area merited setting up a new operation. New Haven's founders had originally envisioned their town as a major trading center, but they had been unsuccessful in realizing that goal. Iron production offered them the prospect of a major export item, and Winthrop's findings were impressive enough that he had little trouble in convincing New Haven's leading citizens to set up an ironworks. The forge and furnace were placed on Farm River near the outlet of present-day Lake Saltonstall in East Haven, and ore was taken from the bogs of North Haven, carried to the works by way of the Quinnipiac River. By the spring of 1657 the furnaces had been fired up; they continued to operate until abandoned near the end of the seventeenth century. Repeated complaints in the town records of unruly workers or failure to pay bills again suggest that failure of the operation was in large measure the result of poor management.

Of the first three attempts to produce iron in New England, only one was a financial success, but in a developing economy the return of profit is only one measure of success. All, however, were important to the region because they provided much needed iron for local use. Demands for iron increased after these beginnings, and many small ironworks sprang up in the last third of the seventeenth century—all of them in southern New England. North Saugus, Concord, Rowley, Westvale, Groton, Pawtucket Falls, and Braintree all had ironworks serving chiefly local markets. The dream of iron becoming a major export was not to be realized.

In terms of techniques and goods produced, manufacturing in New England at the outset of the eighteenth century resembled traditional English manufacturing. By the century's end some of the practices of the Industrial Revolution in Britain had reached New England, and the processes of industrialization, which were to dominate the region's development during the nineteenth century, were already at work in a few areas. Yet we are concerned only with the changes that provided the preconditions for the true industrialization of New England.

Population increase and commercial patterns were basic factors in determining the character of eighteenth-century manufacture in New England. Increasing numbers of colonists eventually brought the region to threshold levels in terms of potential demand and volume. However, entrepreneurial response to the demand was markedly selective. Several factors combined to inhibit development; for example, the population was scattered over a large area, and transportation costs were high. In addition, a lack of currency or exchangeable local commodities in some rural areas produced a generally low effective purchasing power—the cash-deficient economy developed in the seventeenth century had persisted into the eighteenth. The semi-barter nature of that economy proved advantageous to rural areas in which urban mercantile firms sought locally produced commodities, but other areas, with fewer and less valuable products to exchange, were able to purchase little and remained to a large degree locally subsistent.

By mid-eighteenth century an external factor began to affect colonial manufacture. As the British government committed itself more fully to a mercantilistic relationship with the North American colonies, imperial restrictions on colonial manufactures became more frequent and were more effectively enforced. Previously only commerce had been subjected to such regulation, through the various navigation acts. In the hopes of insuring a market solely to British interests or to protect the British market from colonial manufacturers, Parliament forbade colonial manufacture or export of certain goods. It also restricted the colonial use of a few raw materials, such as mast pine. Evasion of many regulations was possible because manpower was never adequate (nor exceptionally loyal to the Crown) and because provincial governors were simply unwilling to interfere with the colonists' activities. In many an instance a Crown official found his life more tolerable if he looked the other way. In New England many eighteenth-century regulations were doubly severe, for they affected not only local production but trade as well. When the Hat Act forbade the export of colonial-made hats to Britain, not only the local hatters in the urban villages suffered, but so did the merchants who were profiting by the trade. While curtailment of the use of the white pine aided the mast-cutters and traders, it had a reverse effect on merchants who were using pipe staves, shingles, and other lumber products as the bases of their overseas trade.

The pattern of manufacturing established by the end of the seventeenth century continued to dominate well into the eighteenth century, with domestic and artisan production remaining the most widespread type of activity. New England was probably not unique among the colonial regions in the amount of domestic manufacture that it turned out, but, because of the group or partial group nature of its settlements, community local-service production was more widely available than in other seaboard regions. Each town attempted to provide its residents with basic services—sawmill, gristmill, fulling mill, tannery, smithy—and many towns were able to achieve such a goal within a few years after initial settlement (with the notable exception of fulling mills). Those activities often created a state of near self-sufficiency; for example, a farmer in the Connecticut Valley claimed that he bought nothing except nails and salt. Goods from household production rarely entered the exchange economy, and imported manufactures were available in urban villages but rare and usually limited to luxury items elsewhere.

In a few instances the crafts of a village artisan might be sold more widely than in the local community, the superiority of the product encouraging its transportation and sale elsewhere, in spite of the added costs. For most products, however, the relationship between quality and range of distribution is unclear. Access to a larger distribution area might have encouraged the manufacturer to produce a better product, one that could compete with the products of more distant manufacturers and thereby justify higher transportation costs. A critical agent in supplying larger access for local goods was the itinerant peddler, who circulating from village to village and among the dispersed farmsteads, became an increasingly important factor in the distribution of lighter consumer and household goods. Eventually known as "Yankee peddlers," such men also roamed outside the New England region to take its many products to an ever larger market.

The basic service manufactures found in the rural towns were also part of the urban village landscape. But during the eighteenth century other manufactures were added to the urban villages. As they expanded their commercial activities and increased in population, economic specialization and division of labor became more characteristic of such centers, while greater demand and purchasing power among the inhabitants also contributed to the diversification of manufactures. Such new manufactures were generally consumer-oriented, direct competitors of goods imported from Britain. By mid-eighteenth century, candlemakers, paper-makers, paper-hangers, glaziers, goldsmiths, silversmiths, lace-makers, and pewterers were among the newer kinds of craftsmen to be found in urban villages such as Boston, Salem, or Hartford. For the most part, the introduction of new activities represented the continuing diffusion of skilled workers, technology, and styles from Great Britain. That diffusion pattern began with Pilgrim settlement and eventually would be responsible for the introduction of the Industrial Revolution into New England.

During the nineteenth century, Lynn, Massachusetts, became one of the leading centers in the women's shoe industry in the United States. In Lynn as in other New England towns, shoes were made at home or by itinerant cobblers; in 1750, however, an emgirant Welsh shoemaker set up shop in the village, divided his operation into several processes, and employed apprentices to work in each process. He decided upon women's shoes as his specialty. Many of his workers eventually migrated to other New England towns and set up firms of their own; thus a successful pattern of operation was carried beyond its point of introduction to the region. Imported skills, technology, reputable entrepreneurship, and specialization were the eighteenth-century contributions to Lynn's nine-teenth-century industrial enterprises, just as they were to other indus-tries throughout southern New England.

Another manufacture which rose to prominence during the early dec-ades of the eighteenth century was the production of men's beaver hats; this an early example of the colonists making a better and cheaper prod-uct than did their British counterparts. Initially the activity was loosely tied to the nearly defunct beaver fur trade of earlier times, for many of the first hatters were found in towns where that trade had focused. That historic connection became less important, however, as the regional sup-ply of beaver pelts declined. The hatters then chose to locate where there was market and a supply of imported pelts, probably from Albany. At first, production was for local wearers, but by the eighteenth century the hatters had found a brisk market for their beaver-felt hats in Eu-rope, where production costs were considerably higher. By 1730, British hatters, outraged by the successful invasion and capture of their markets by the colonials, were protesting to Parliament and demanding legisla-tion that would curtail colonial competition. In 1732 Parliament re-sponded with the passage of the Hat Act, which forbade the export of colonial-made hats from one colony to another or overseas; it also lim-ited each colonial hatter to two apprentices in the hopes of further limit-ing growth. Thus the thriving beaver-felt hat manufacture, which was centered mainly in southern New England and the city of New York, be-came one of the first colonial enterprises to be subjected to imperial restrictions. They successfully curtailed expansion into the overseas mar-ket, but it is difficult to ascribe that curtailment solely to imperial con-trol because growth of local markets and increased difficulties (importa-tion of pelts and consequent higher costs) may have forced the colonial hatters to withdraw from the British market even if the government had not intervened.

Both the shoe- and hat-making enterprises were ones whose locations were determined by local domestic needs or the presence of skilled workers. Other types of manufacture such as ironworks or wood-works were located on the basis of available raw material. While these enter-prises were less consequential as antecedents for nineteenth-century in-dustry, several were of inestimable importance to life in eighteenth-century New England. At the end of the seventeenth century there were six ironworks in the region, all of which were probably simple forges and furnaces. By 1731 iron production had expanded and diversified to six furnaces, nineteen bloomery forges, and one slitting mill. Construction of more forges, furnaces, and specialized mills continued during the remaining decades of the century, so that on the eve of the Revolutionary War, Massachusetts ranked third among the North American colonies in the number of forges and furnaces—outranked only by Pennsylvania and Maryland in the number of furnaces and by Pennsylvania and New Jersey in the number of forges. Annexation of Plymouth Colony into Massachusetts in 1691 contributed greatly to Massachusetts' ranking for most of the ironworks were concentrated in the towns of the absorbed colony. Iron production relied heavily on bog ores as it did in the seventeenth century, but hematite ores from western New England were used more increasingly as the century progressed and the bog deposits were depleted.

It has already been noted that successful ironmaking in southern Massachusetts was associated with astute management. Another major factor in that success, however, was the area's proximity to the two major commercial areas of southern New England, Massachusetts Bay and Narragansett Bay. Still, regional production was inadequate to meet demands, and pig iron had to be regularly imported from Pennsylvania, the Chesapeake Bay region, and New Jersey to supplement local production and to provide varieties of iron that the bog ores did not yield.

Exploitation of the rock hematite ores of western New England began shortly after 1730, when New York interests led by the Livingston family started mining ore at Salisbury, Connecticut, on the southern fringe of the Berkshire hills. A western or New York focus on that area continued for three decades, until a road that allowed ores and pig iron to move to southeastern New England was finally cut through from Hartford. Salisbury then became a rival to southeastern Massachusetts as the leading center of pig iron production.

In 1750, iron manufacture in the American colonies came under the total regulation of the British government. A parliamentary act of that year was a compromise between various pressure groups who on the one hand feared the encouragement of manufactures in the colonies lest they compete with established British interests and on the other desired to break Britain's dependence on imported Swedish bar iron. The act had two major sections. One ended all customs and duties on pig iron imported from the colonies but permitted the free importation of bar iron to London only. Further, bar iron brought to London could not be carried more than a ten-mile radius from the city, except to Royal Navy

IRON-MAKING

A blacksmith forge of the type shown here from Diderot's *Encyclopédie* could be found almost anywhere a skilled blacksmith was at work. The many tools used in the trade are scattered about the shed and even hang from the rafters. Note the large leather bellows, which was used to force air into the fire to create the intense heat that softened the iron.

In a hammer-mill a gigantic wooden hammer flattened iron bars into thinner sheets, from which latches, nails, tools, and other things could be easily shaped. (*Columbia University Libraries*)

yards. This, it was hoped, would stimulate colonial export production, an expectation that went mainly unrealized, for local American demands continued to consume most colonial output. The second part of the act dealt with the secondary processing of iron and, if enforced, would have virtually curtailed the production of various types of iron and steel. After June 24, 1750, no establishment or equipment to process iron beyond the bar-iron stage could be erected legally in the colonies. The works prohibited were (1) slitting mills, which made iron for nails, (2) plating forges, which hammered sheet and tin-plate iron, and (3) steel furnaces. Colonial governors were instructed to report to London the number of such plants in existence at the time. Historian Arthur Bining has concluded that the number reported underestimated the actual establishments, the first instance of colonial disregard for the act. Fortunately for later colonial metallurgical developments, the act was widely disobeyed and circumvented throughout the colonies, often with the discreet approval of the governors, who found it more to their advantage to placate the colonists than to report accurately to London. One important effect of the act was to make the colonists more aware of the underdog position in which mercantilism placed them.

Secondary iron processing was found at many sites throughout the older settled areas of New England. It has been noted that such enterprises were part of the complex of activities which focused on the main centers of shipbuilding. By 1750 ironmasters, concentrated in the eastern Connecticut towns of Woodstock, Norwich, Plainfield, Stonington, Groton, New London, Saybrook, and Killingworth, were specializing in plating mills to produce sheet iron for copperers, whitesmiths, and tinsmiths. During the Revolutionary War only the producers in the coastal towns burned by the British experienced any discontinuity in their operations. Thus the continued presence of skilled metallurgists after the war fostered the development of the area into one characterized by highly specialized metal products during the nineteenth century, a tradition which has continued to the present day.

The development of the Hope Furnace in Rhode Island illustrates specifically an important aspect of late colonial manufacture in New England, the strengthening ties between commerce and manufacture. As New England's overseas commerce became more and more complex, and the volume and variety of unprocessed staples decreased, merchants began to turn to local manufactures. Iron was one commodity with sufficient demand in local, regional, intercolonial, and overseas trade to attract the attention of merchants with capital to speculate in production. Intent on challenging the commercial hegemony of Newport, a Providence merchant firm, the Brown Brothers, already the largest colonial producer of spermaceti candles and owner of several rum distilleries, decided to venture into ironmaking—probably not too speculative a venture, for by then iron had been produced for many years in the Narragansett region and adjacent parts of southern Massachusetts. The brothers built their furnace at Pawatuck and named it the Hope Furnace. Ore came from local bogs, but charcoal was less easy to come by: the surrounding countryside was chiefly farmland, and the Browns were unable to acquire the large wooded properties needed for a continuing supply of charcoal. Instead they contracted with nearby farmers to supply wood from their woodlots. Some skilled labor was hired from Salisbury and other workers were lured away from the furnaces of southeastern Massachusetts, another example of how skills spread in colonial times.

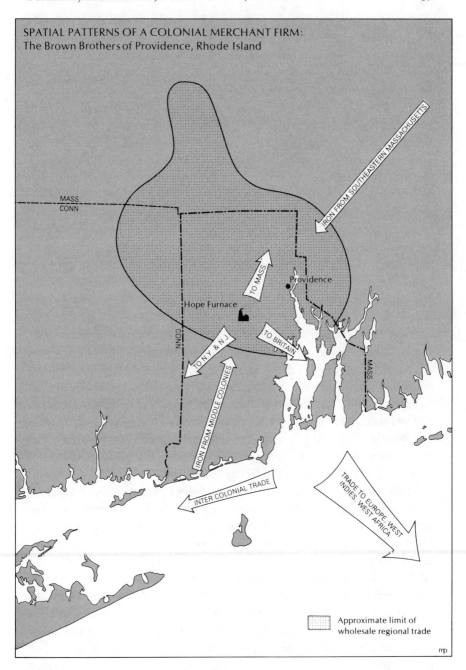

SPATIAL PATTERNS OF A COLONIAL MERCHANT FIRM:
The Brown Brothers of Providence, Rhode Island

Figure 5-1.

By 1767 the Hope furnace was producing iron in sufficient quantity for a small shipment of pig iron to be sent to England, which in turn financed British goods, which were then shipped to the Browns. The pattern was repeated for the remainder of the colonial era, so that the Browns succeeded where other New Englanders had failed—they used exported iron as the basis of trade with Britain. A historian of the firm, however, has concluded that New York was the principal market for the furnace's output. Interestingly enough, the chief buyer in New York was a merchant-manufacturer, specializing in a variety of cast-iron products. But iron from the Hope Furnace was distributed more widely than just to Britain or New York (see Fig. 5-1). It was sent to forges in Massachusetts, Connecticut, New Jersey, and Pennsylvania. To make certain types of iron, pigs with different characteristics were imported to mix with local production, so that the lines of transportation that moved Hope pigs also returned large quantities of iron. Iron from the Hibernia Furnace in northern New Jersey and the Livington's Ancram Furnace in the Hudson Valley were the principal sources of the iron used in the blending.

Many years before the hematite ores of western Connecticut were found, another metal was being taken from those hills. In 1705 at Simsbury a rich vein of copper was discovered. Two years later a mine was opened which over the decades became a labyrinth of tunnels and chambers, for underground rather than open-pit was the extraction method used. The ore, originally assayed at fifteen per cent copper, provided most of the copper used in eighteenth-century Connecticut and surrounding colonies, in spite of imperial restrictions forbidding the processing of copper ore in the North American colonies.

Neither Puritan tenets nor emigration dulled the appetites of Englishmen overseas for alcoholic beverages. By 1700, cider had replaced beer as the most popular colonial beverage. Apples were then widespread and less malting barley was grown. A cider press thus became as indispensable locally as a gristmill or a sawmill. Then, early in the eighteenth century cider's popularity—particularly in the larger urban villages—was challenged by rum. Rum, as we have seen, was made from molasses imported from the West Indies. Apparently little was consumed locally at first, and for some time rum remained an item of commerce for European markets and the African slave trade. Exactly when and how it became a popular beverage in New England is a topic that awaits further study. But by the second decade of the eighteenth century numerous rum distilleries had been built in and around the urban villages trading with the West Indies—and there were few that did not trade there. As the leading port, Boston maintained over a dozen distilleries. In many cases the owners of the distilleries were local merchants heavily involved in overseas trade and, like their counterparts, the Browns of Providence, sought manufactured items as staples for that trade.

Communications

The dispersed character of the original English settlements made the need for effective communication among them an immediate problem, the dimensions of which increased as settlement expanded into new areas and as the settlers' activities became more numerous and varied. At first, waterways provided the principal means of trade and communication among the scattered settlements and with the frontier. Even before settlement, coastal waters and streams had been used by explorers and traders. After settlement, water transportation became a mainstay of the region's communication network, a status it continued to enjoy until railroads emerged as the chief mode of intra-regional linkages. Meanwhile a crude system of roads slowly developed to service places lacking water transportation.

As the settlements' economies progressed from the highly subsistent frontier stage to more commercial oriented production, the role of water transport in carriage of heavy or bulk items was intensified. For example, in the forest-oriented manufactures of the lower Piscataqua River, water transportation was essential to the entire operation, from the floating of newly cut logs to mills to the shipment of finished products to markets; only as cutting areas were depleted and moved further inland did roads start to become important. Similarly, the movement of timber and naval stores from southern Maine depended almost exclusively on water transport. Grains and forest products from the immediate hinterlands of the many small ports dotting the coastline from Connecticut to Maine moved to wharfside by road or path but then were absorbed into the coastwide trade. Many of those ports literally owed their existence to that trade. Bulk commodities from the Connecticut Valley moved downriver to port, and as long as cartage to port was impossible or prohibitively expensive, the river remained a principal routeway. Below the falls above Windsor, the boats used in shipping were often seaworthy, carrying goods not only downstream but also to and from Boston. Even such small streams as the Sudbury and Concord rivers near Boston were occasionally used for transport. Many a fledgling manufacture depended on water transport to bring its raw materials together, as exemplified in the ironworks at Saugus and East Haven.

Meanwhile, land circulation patterns were being developed. Indian trails were the first corridors of land movement; the Pilgrims used them in their first surveys of Cape Cod, as did settlers moving into the interior. But the trails eventually proved to be less serviceable to the colonists than to the Indians. Colonial patterns of movement did not always follow those of the natives; more important, however, were the differing characteristics of the movement itself. Where the Indians traveled unencumbered on foot, the colonists wanted corridors suitable for beasts and cargoes as well as men. The technology of road building that the colonists brought with them was rather crude—roads in England were still often impassable in bad weather and rough even under the best conditions—but in colonial New England the application of even those standards was probably impossible.

In colonial times many aspects of livelihood had to be undertaken almost simultaneously, and a chronic labor shortage existed. There simply was not enough manpower or time available to do everything, and road building, however important it was recognized to be, did not enjoy the highest priority: housing construction, field workings, and domestic manufactures were among the activities which received more immediate attention and time. The need for adequate roads was readily acknowledged by the colonists, and numerous authorizations by colonial assemblies to build or to improve roads attest to this. In an effort to encourage the development of an intracolonial trunk highway system, the colonies began to designate certain town roads as king's or queen's highways, but little was actually done to improve the condition of the roads so-designated. Thus, throughout the colonial era the condition of a road depended more on the nature of the soil in the roadbed and the vagaries of weather than on the desires or nomenclature of men.

While colonial assemblies authorized road building or improvement, in New England the actual construction of roads was the responsibility of the individual towns. Each male resident of a town was expected to give a few days labor annually toward the upkeep and construction of roads within his town; however, few townsmen complied with town regulations in that regard. The penalty for not doing so was usually a small fine, which was rarely collected even when it was imposed. Further, the question of rights-of-way was ambiguous. Few towns laid out rights-of-way for roads or paths, and landowners objected to later appropriation of their properties and sometimes went so far as to include road-beds within their fenced fields—horses and men might jump the fences but wagons or carts could not. Also, many early road layouts emphasized linking points within the town, not connecting adjoining towns. That system was consistent with the town focus of colonial New England, but it was not the most effective means to produce rapidly an integrated intracolonial or intercolonial road system.

Against this background the physical environment of New England presented transportation obstacles that were impossible to overcome in the seventeenth century. The numerous streams or inlets between the peninsulas required bridges or ferries if the roadways were to be usable year-round. Yet, because bridges were expensive to build, required large numbers of men for construction and repairs, and were apt to be dam-aged by floods and ice, it is not surprising that their construction was limited and even vehemently opposed in some towns. As an alternative, ferries were also expensive but could provide a small revenue if they were leased on concession or if a fee was charged of users. They were established at important crossings—at the mouth of the Connecticut River, and at Hartford, Boston, and Portsmouth. In Rhode Island there was no choice but to maintain ferries between the settlements on the islands of Narragansett Bay and the mainland. The embayed character of much of the eastern coast meant that land routes between the coastal settlements were less direct than water routes; further, in many coastal areas (and often adjacent to streams) tidal marshes and swamps made the construction of roadbeds impossible. Away from the coast the nu-merous glacial bogs and surrounding unfirm land posed comparable problems for road building. The rocky outcrops of the uplands and the steep slopes of hills were problems of another sort, but no less signifi-cant as obstacles for road builders.

Despite the obstacles of limited technology, labor allocation, and physical environment, the colonists slowly began to develop a crude road system. Paths or trails were fairly easy to mark out in cleared areas or where burning had cleared the forest of ground cover, so that move-ment of men on foot was relatively simple. Each new settlement also was connected by a path or trail to an older town center. Eventually many of those trails were widened—by the dual track made by cart wheels and by further clearing. Yet tree stumps were left to rot in the roadbeds, and these and other hazards—holes left by rotted stumps, half-buried rocks, ruts cut by running water, and surfaces broken by hooves of animals made the roads barely passable much of the time.

A series of Indian trails provided the basic network of an intercolonial road system in southern New England. Settlers who first emigrated to the Connecticut Valley chose as a route of entry the Great Trail. Beginning at Watertown in the Bay Colony, the trail ran to Sudbury and then wound its way around ponds and bogs and over hills and rocky outcrops to a point near Springfield. There it crossed the Connecticut, linking with another trail that ran along the west bank of the river. That route remained the major trunk connection between the Massachusetts section of the Valley and the Bay towns throughout the colonial era, but it was throughout the seventeenth century unsuitable for vehicular traffic. Brookfield was its main way-station. A more direct route between Hartford and the Bay settlements was developed south of the Great Trail. At Mendon one branch of the new trail went west to Hartford, while another continued south to Providence and Rhode Island. Along the coast the settlements east of the mouth of the Connecticut River were linked to the river settlements by the Pequot Trail. There, too, a series of droving routes centered on New London was in use by the end of the seventeenth century. West of the river, road conditions as late as the Revolutionary War, if some travelers are to be believed, were so poor that travelers to New York preferred to ferry to Long Island and then continue to New York.

Travelers' accounts often provide more information about the actual status of the colonial road system than do references in town or provincial records. Two items from the first decade of the eighteenth century illustrate what the colonists had been able to accomplish by that time. Judge Sewall recorded in his diary that the body of a Jew living in Boston who died in February, 1703, was expeditiously transported by coach to Bristol and then by ferry to the Jewish cemetery at Newport, Rhode Island, within the twenty-four hour period required for proper burial by the tenets of his religion. The journal of a trip which Madame Knight of Boston took in late fall and early winter 1704–5 from Boston to New York and back describes vividly the traveling conditions of the period. While her descriptions of roads and accommodations leave the modern reader with a dismal picture of eighteenth-century travel in New England, they differ little from contemporary travel descriptions in England or France. Dirty inns, poor roads, delays in meeting the postmen who were to accompany her, horses falling on poorly repaired bridges, ferries being nearly upturned by sudden squalls, and dangerous fords were among the trials she had to endure; most of those problems would be in existence more than a century later for future travelers to grapple with.

For example, between New London and Saybrook she found "The Rodes all along this way are very bad, Incumbred with Rocks and mountainos passages, wch were very disagreeable to my tired carcass." Many colonial roads were not linked, and Madame Knight and her companion discovered this after spending several hours searching down a country lane for the continuing main road. Still, it is remarkable that within a few decades of settlement the colonists had developed a road system adequate enough for a virtually unattended woman to make a long journey safely—even being spared one of the dangers of European travel, highway bandits.

The third quarter of the eighteenth century saw many changes in the colonies, but few of those changes involved the road network. James Birket is less well known than his contemporary European travelers (such as Peter Kalm or Andrew Burnaby) in mid-eighteenth century, but his journal is probably the best geographic document for New England because of the extensive quantity of material he recorded and the interrelationships which he perceived in the landscape. For example, while traveling along the Piscataqua he observed the effects of settlement and deforestation on the lumber enterprises of the lower river—especially that the areas in which logs were cut were increasingly distant from the river and that the timber had to be carted to the riverbank before being floated downstream to Portsmouth. Birket may have been prejudiced, but he nonetheless felt that the Portsmouth shipyards used inferior timbers for ships sold to overseas buyers. Of the road system of New England he judged the better roads to be in the older coastal towns, even describing the route from Newbury to Salem via Ipswich as an "excellent road." In Connecticut he had few kind comments to make about the roads, but evidently he did not have to search for trunk roads as did Madame Knight. Intracolonial and intercolonial linkages were probably well advanced beyond what they were at the beginning of the century. Of the roads east of the Connecticut River, "stony" and "uneven" were the words used most frequently to describe them, but he had far stronger language for the roads west of the river. Between Norwalk and Fairfield was a "Most Intollerable bad road," and near the New York border he traversed "3 Miles of Most miserable road." By the time of the Revolution little change could be noted in New England's communications network—overland routes between the principal urban villages were laid out and generally usable, and more roads or pathways spread into the interior from the older settlements, but the condition of roadbeds varied greatly from place to place. It was possible for an in-

dividual to move on horseback with a fair amount of ease; animals could
be driven from place to place. But waterways and coastal movements
would reign supreme until challenged by the railroad in the nineteenth
century.

Suggested References

Albion, Robert G. *Forest and Sea Power: The Timber Problem of the
Royal Navy 1652–1862* (Cambridge, Mass.: Harvard University Press,
1926).

Bailyn, Bernard and Lottc. *Massachusetts Shipping 1697–1714: A Statistical Study* (Cambridge, Mass.: Harvard University Press, 1959).

Birket, James. *Some Cursory Remarks* (New Haven, Conn.: Yale University Press, 1916).

Black, Robert C. *The Younger John Winthrop* (New York: Columbia
University Press, 1966).

Bridenbaugh, Carl. *The Colonial Craftsman* (Chicago: University of
Chicago Press, 1961).

Briggs, L. Vernon. *History of Shipbuilding on North River.* (Boston:
Coburn Brothers, 1889).

Calder, Isabel. *The New Haven Colony* (New Haven: Yale University
Press, 1934).

Clark, Victor S. *History of Manufactures in the United States 1607–1860*
(Washington, D.C.: Carnegie Institution, 1916).

Hartley, E. N. *Ironworks on the Saugus* (Norman, Okla.: University of
Oklahoma Press, 1957).

Hedges, James B. *The Browns of Providence Plantations: Colonial Years*
(Cambridge, Mass.: Harvard University Press, 1952).

Knight, Sarah K. *Journal of Madame Knight* (Boston: David R. Godine,
1972).

Malone, Joseph J. *Pine Trees and Politics: The Naval Stores and Forest
Policy in Colonial New England 1691–1775* (Seattle, Wash.: University of Washington Press, 1964).

Mitchell, Isabel S. *Roads and Road-Making in Colonial Connecticut*
(New Haven, Conn.: Yale University Press for Connecticut Tercentenary Commission, 1933).

Saltonstall, William G. *Ports of Piscataqua* (Cambridge, Mass.: Harvard
University Press, 1941).

EPILOGUE

The immediate effects of the Revolutionary War on the geography of New England were generally minimal. Battles in the region were few, and British occupation of some coastal sites was brief. The impact of raids by pro-British Indians on the frontier settlements was generally less devastating than comparable attacks during the colonial imperial wars. The British burned several villages and town centers along Long Island Sound, but they were quickly restored after the war. Disruption of New England's overseas commerce was another matter, however, and had a severe effect on the regional economy. Trade with Britain, of course, was cut off. While temporary trade with Britain's enemies (France, Spain, and their colonies) filled the void somewhat, in general the wartime dislocation was such that the prewar patterns were never totally restored—a crushing blow to the region considering that commerce was one of the few dynamic aspects of New England's late colonial economy.

During the postwar decades New England remained in the preconditions for take-off stage, and moved into the next stage in Rostow's model —take-off—only after the introduction of industry in the early nineteenth century. The dichotomy between interior and northern New England— characterized as rural and agricultural—and coastal and southern New England—marked by urbanization, commerce, and linkages beyond the region—had evolved during the eighteenth century and was accentuated by the introduction of industry to the latter areas. Industry and its associated activities would ultimately transform many aspects of the colonial

landscape. Colonial commerce and manufacture were important antecedents of many nineteenth-century industries, and the impact of industry was greater in southern New England, where such activities were
more prosperous. In contrast northern New England was more selectively
affected by industrialization, and it has maintained into the twentieth
century picturesque villages and the image of pleasant ruralism.

Urbanism was an important aspect of colonial New England, and during the nineteenth century, urbanization increased and took on several
new dimensions. With increased population the colonial urban villages
became cities. It was the era of the rise of the industrial city, a new type
of urbanism for New England. As industry became more and more dominant its prominence as the principal urbanizing process grew. The
urbanized areas affected in some instances were colonial villages, town
centers, or communities; in other cases they were entirely new centers,
such as Lowell or Naugatuck. The new massing of people in southeastern New England was around the shoe and textile industries, while in
southwestern New England much of the massing was attached to centers
of colonially developed crafts and skills. In the new setting of expanding
industrialization and urbanism, Boston regained its status as the regional metropolis and also regained the regional dominance it had enjoyed during the seventeenth and early eighteenth century.

Independence gave New England a new and less restrictive political
context. As a major region of the new and expanding country, it was
able to broaden its resource base, the range of its markets, and the scope
of its intellectual, political, and economic influences—but only when the
political separatism of the colonial era had been subdued by a growing
sense of nationalism. Still, amalgamation of the region and the nation
had its negative consequences, which especially affected commerce and
agriculture. But the growth of a new nationalism taught New Englanders that regional prosperity required a balance of positive and negative factors.

The rising percentage of urbanized population was, of course, at the
expense of a decreasing rural population, another regional characteristic
which had its origin in the colonial period. Throughout the colonial era
dissatisfied rural New Englanders could either stay put or migrate to
more desirable regions. Industrialization presented a third option—migration to the region's growing cities. Some native New Englanders took
that option, but many more chose to emigrate to other areas of the
United States, transplanting many of their cultural patterns. Such mi-

gration had begun before the Revolutionary War; thus postwar migrations represented an intensification of the pattern rather than an innovation in the new economic stage. Similarly, the agricultural problems of the late colonial period carried over into the new economic stage. And a new factor was added, competition from agricultural areas west of the Appalachians. But agricultural specializations—onions and tobacco in the Connecticut Valley for example—survived profitably, while the growth of cities helped to revive some urban-oriented production, such as truck-gardening and dairying, in tributary areas.

Meanwhile urban centers were expanding rapidly, and their population characteristics were changing. Foreign, non-English immigrants settled mainly in the growing cities rather than in rural areas. The once-dominant "Englishness" of the region was steadily diluted as Irish, Italians, Portuguese, Armenians, and others arrived. Ethnic changes in the urban population further highlighted the difference between industrial urbanism and rural areas, where (except along the Quebéc border) the population remained predominantly of colonial English or Anglo-Celtic background. Such a situation—like other aspects of a region's past and present—serves to emphasize that rates of geographic change are rarely uniform throughout a region and that aspects of earlier geographic features linger on even when significant changes take place. The post-colonial scene had many new features, some startlingly new, but as with any developmental continuum it was a combination of heritage and innovation.

BIBLIOGRAPHY

This bibliography reports only a small portion of the literature on colonial New England, a literature so vast that a comprehensive listing would probably be longer than this book. The items cited below are offered as a guide to some of the more widely available pieces of that literature in the hopes that the readers will pursue topics of interest. Periodical articles have not been included unless the topic is not covered adequately elsewhere, and only a few town histories whose texts are relevantly geographic have been included. The best secondary monographs have valuable bibliographies of their own. Primary unpublished sources are not listed, although they are the basic sources on which all studies of the region must begin. Space does not permit their inclusion here. Unpublished records of various sorts exist for most New England towns, and other types of research materials may be found in many excellent regional historical and archival depositories such as the Massachusetts Historical Society, the Massachusetts Archives, the Newport Historical Society, the Essex Institute, and the Connecticut State Library. Outside of the region the New York Public Library, the Library of Congress, the Clements Library in Ann Arbor, Michigan, the Newberry Library in Chicago, and the Huntington Library in San Marino, California, are only a few of the national treasure troves that contain copious amounts of material on New England.

Albion, Robert G. *Forest and Sea Power: The Timber Problem of the Royal Navy 1652–1862* (Cambridge, Mass.: Harvard University Press, 1926).

American Husbandry. Ed. Harry J. Carman. (New York: Columbia University Press, 1939).

Andrews, Charles M. *The Beginnings of Connecticut 1632–1662* (New Haven, Conn.: Yale University Press for Connecticut Tercentenary Commission, 1934).

————. *The Colonial Period of American History.* Vols. 1 & 2: "The Settlements" (New Haven, Conn.: Yale University Press, 1934–36).

————. *The Rise and Fall of the New Haven Colony* (New Haven, Conn.: Yale University Press for Connecticut Tercentenary Commission, 1936).

Arber, E. (ed.). *Travels and Works of Captain John Smith.* 2 vols. (Edinburgh: John Grant, 1910).

Ayres, Harral. *The Great Trail of New England* (Boston: Meador Publishing Co., 1940).

Bailyn, Bernard. *The New England Merchants in the Seventeenth Century* (Cambridge, Mass.: Harvard University Press, 1955).

Bailyn, Bernard and Lotte. *Massachusetts Shipping 1697–1714: A Statistical Study* (Cambridge, Mass.: Harvard University Press, 1959).

Barber, John W. *Connecticut Historical Collections* (New Haven, Conn.: Durrie & Peck, 1836).

————. *Massachusetts Historical Collections* (Worcester, Mass.: Dorr, Howland, & Co., 1839).

Baxter, James P. (ed.). *The Trelawny Papers.* Vol. III of "Documentary History of Maine." (Portland, Maine: Hoyt, Fogg, Donham, 1884).

————. *Sir Ferdinando Gorges and His Province of Maine.* 3 vols. (Boston: Prince Society, 1890).

Bidwell, Percy W., and Falconer, John I. *History of Agriculture in the Northern United States 1620–1860* (Washington, D.C.: Carnegie Institution, 1925).

Bining, Arthur C. *British Regulation of the Colonial Iron Industry* (Philadelphia: University of Pennsylvania, 1933).

Birket, James. *Some Cursory Remarks* (New Haven, Conn.: Yale University Press, 1916).

Black, Robert C. *The Younger John Winthrop* (New York: Columbia University Press, 1966).

Bradford, William. *History of Plymouth Plantation 1620–1647.* 2 vols. (Boston: Massachusetts Historical Society, 1912).

Bridenbaugh, Carl. *Cities in Revolt* (New York: Capricorn Books, 1964).

————. *Cities in the Wilderness* (New York: Alfred A. Knopf, 1955).

————. *The Colonial Craftsman* (Chicago: University of Chicago Press, 1961).

Briggs, L. Vernon. *History of Shipbuilding on North River* (Boston: Coburn Brothers, 1889).

Brown, Alexander. *The Genesis of the United States.* 2 vols. (New York: Russell & Russell, 1964).

Brown, Ralph H. *Historical Geography of the United States* (New York: Harcourt, Brace and Company, 1948).

Bowen, Clarence W. *The Boundary Disputes of Connecticut* (Boston: James R. Osgood, 1882).

Bowen, Richard L. *Early Rehoboth.* 3 vols. (Rehoboth, Mass.: privately printed, 1946).

Burnaby, Andrew. *Travels Through the Middle Settlements in North-America in the Years 1759 and 1760.* 2nd Ed. (Ithaca, N.Y.: Cornell University Press, 1960).

Bushman, Richard L. *From Puritan to Yankee: Character and Social Order in Connecticut 1690–1765* (Cambridge, Mass.: Harvard University Press, 1967).

Calder, Isabel. *The New Haven Colony* (New Haven, Conn.: Yale University Press, 1934).

Carroll, Peter N. *Puritanism and the Wilderness* (New York: Columbia University Press, 1969).

Cassedy, James H. *Demography in Early America: Beginnings of the Statistical Mind 1600–1800* (Cambridge, Mass.: Harvard University Press, 1969).

A Century of Population Growth (Washington, D.C.: U.S. Government Printing Office, 1909).

Clark, Andrew H. *Acadia: The Geography of Early Nova Scotia to 1760* (Madison, Wisc.: University of Wisconsin Press, 1968).

Clark, Charles E. *The Eastern Frontier: The Settlement of Northern New England 1610–1763* (New York: Alfred A. Knopf, 1970).

Clark, Victor S. *History of Manufactures in the United States 1607–1860* (Washington, D.C.: Carnegie Institution, 1916).

Coleman, Peter J. *The Transformation of Rhode Island 1790–1860* (Providence, R.I.: Brown University Press, 1963).

Cummings, Abbott L. (ed.). *Rural Household Inventories* (Boston: Society for the Preservation of New England Antiquities, 1964).

Deming, Dorothy. *Settlement of Litchfield* (New Haven, Conn.: Yale University Press for Connecticut Tercentenary Commission, 1933).

———. *The Settlement of the Connecticut Towns* (New Haven, Conn.: Yale University Press for Connecticut Tercentenary Commission, 1933).

Dexter, H. M. (ed.). *Mourt's Relation or a Journal of the Plantation at Plymouth* (Boston: John K. Wiggin, 1865).

Douglass, William. *A Summary, Historical and Political, of the First Planting, Progressive Improvements, and Present State of the British Settlements in North-America.* 2 vols. (Boston: n.p., 1760).

Downing, Antoinette F., and Scully, Vincent J. *The Architectural Heritage of Newport, Rhode Island, 1640–1915.* 2nd Ed. (New York: Bramhall House, 1967).

Early Coastwise and Foreign Shipping of Salem (Salem, Mass.: Essex Institute, 1934).

Eliot, Jared. *Essays Upon Field Husbandry in New England* (New York: Columbia University Press, 1934).

Friis, Herman R. "A Series of Population Maps of the Colonies and the United States, 1625–1790" (*Geographical Review*, XXX (July 1940), 463–70).

Felt, Joseph B. *Annals of Salem.* 2 vols. (Salem, Mass.: W. & S. B. Ives, 1845–49).

Ganong, W. F. *Crucial Maps in the Early Cartography and Place-Nomen-*

clature of the Atlantic Coast of Canada (Toronto: University of Toronto Press, 1964).

Gipson, Lawrence H. *The Coming of the Revolution 1763–1775* (New York: Harper & Brothers, 1954).

Glass, D. V., and Eversley, D. E. C. (eds.). *Population in History* (Chicago: Aldine Publishing Co., 1965).

Grant, Charles S. *Democracy in the Connecticut Frontier Town of Kent* (New York: Columbia University Press, 1961).

Green, Constance McL. *History of Naugatuck, Connecticut* (New Haven, Conn.: Yale University Press, 1948).

Greene, Evarts B., and Harrington, Virginia D. *American Population Before the Federal Census of 1790* (Gloucester, Mass.: Peter Smith, 1966).

Greene, Jack P. (ed.). *The American Colonies in the Eighteenth Century 1689–1763* (New York: Appleton, Century Crofts, 1969).

Greene, Lorenzo J. *The Negro in Colonial New England 1620–1776* (New York: Columbia University Press, 1942).

Greven, Philip J., Jr. *Four Generations: Population, Land, and Family in Colonial Andover, Massachusetts* (Ithaca, N.Y.: Cornell University Press, 1970).

Haller, William H., Jr. *The Puritan Frontier: Town-Planting in New England Colonial Development 1630–1660* (New York: Columbia University Press, 1951).

Hartley, E. N. *Ironworks on the Saugus* (Norman, Okla.: University of Oklahoma Press, 1957).

Hedges, James B. *The Browns of Providence Plantations: Colonial Years* (Cambridge, Mass.: Harvard University Press, 1952).

Historical Statistics of the United States (Washington, D.C.: U.S. Government Printing Office, 1960).

Hoadly, Charles J. (ed.). *The Public Records of the Colony of Connecticut.* 15 vols. (Hartford, Conn.: Case, Lockwood & Brainard Co., 1850–90).

Hofstader, Richard. *America at 1750: A Social Portrait* (New York: Alfred A. Knopf, 1971).

Holbrook, Stewart H. *The Yankee Exodus* (New York: Macmillan, 1950).

Hooker, Roland M. *The Colonial Trade of Connecticut* (New Haven, Conn.: Yale University Press for Connecticut Tercentenary Commission, 1936).

Hutchinson, Thomas. *The History of the Colony and Province of Massachusetts-Bay.* 3 vols. (Cambridge, Mass.: Harvard University Press, 1936).

James, Sydney V. (ed.). *Three Visitors to Early Plymouth* (Plymouth, Mass.: Plymouth Plantation, 1963).

Jameson, J. Franklin (ed.). *Johnson's Wonder-Working Providence 1628–1651* (New York: Charles Scribner's Sons, 1910).

Jenness, John S. *The Isles of Shoals* (New York: Hurd and Houghton, 1873).

Jewett, Amos E. *Rowley, Massachusetts* (Rowley, Mass.: Privately printed, 1946).

Jones, Mary J. A. *Congregational Commonwealth: Connecticut 1636–1662* (Middletown, Conn.: Wesleyan University Press, 1968).

Josselyn, John. *An Account of Two Voyages to New England* (London: G. Widdowes, 1675. Reprinted in Massachusetts Historical Society *Collections*, 3rd series, III (1833), 211–397).

————. *New England's Rarities* (London: G. Widdowes, 1672. Reprinted in *Archaeologia Americana*, IV (1860), 133–238).

Judd, Sylvester. *History of Hadley* (Springfield, Mass.: H. R. Huntting & Co., 1905).

Keith, Herbert C., and Harte, Charles R. *The Early Iron Industry of Connecticut*. (New Haven, Conn.: Mack and Noel, 1936).

Kimball, Gertrude S. *Providence in Colonial Times* (Boston: Houghton Mifflin, 1912).

Labaree, Benjamin W. *Patriots and Partisans: The Merchants of Newburyport 1764–1815* (Cambridge, Mass.: Harvard University Press, 1962).

Labaree, Leonard W. *Milford, Connecticut* (New Haven, Conn.: Yale University Press for Connecticut Tercentenary Commission, 1933).

Langdon, G. D. *Plymouth Colony: A History of New Plymouth 1620–1691* (New Haven, Conn.: Yale University Press, 1966).

Leach, Douglas E. *The Northern Colonial Frontier 1607–1763* (New York: Holt, Rinehart, and Winston, 1966).

LeBlanc, Robert G. *Location of Manufacturing in New England in the 19th Century*. Number 7 of "Geography Publications at Dartmouth" (Hanover, N.H.: Dartmouth College Geography Department, 1969).

Lee, W. Storrs. *The Yankees of Connecticut* (New York: Henry Holt & Co., 1957).

Levermore, Charles H. (ed.). *Forerunners and Competitors of the Pilgrims and Puritans*. 2 vols. (Brooklyn, N.Y.: New England Society of Brooklyn, 1912).

Lockridge, Kenneth A. *A New England Town, the First Hundred Years: Dedham Massachusetts, 1636–1736* (New York: W. W. Norton, 1970).

————. "The Population of Dedham, Massachusetts, 1636–1736" *Economic History Review*, 2nd Series, XIX (1966), 318–344).

Love, William D. *The Colonial History of Hartford Gathered from the Original Records* (Hartford, Conn.: by author, 1914).

McFarland, Raymond. *A History of the New England Fisheries* (New York: D. Appleton and Company, 1911).

McManis, Douglas R. *European Impressions of the New England Coast 1497–1620* (Chicago: University of Chicago Department of Geography Research Series, 1972).

————. "The Traditions of Vinland" (*Annals* of the Association of American Geographers, LIX (December 1969), 797–814).

Malone, Joseph L. *Pine Trees and Politics: The Naval Stores and Forest Policy in Colonial New England 1691–1775* (Seattle, Wash.: University of Washington Press, 1964).

Mathews, Lois K. *The Expansion of New England* (Boston: Houghton Mifflin, 1909).

Maverick, Samuel. "A Briefe Discription of New England and the Severall

Townes Therein" (Massachusetts Historical Society *Proceedings*, 2nd Series, I (1884–85), 231–49).

Miner, Sidney H., and Stanton, George D. (eds.). *The Diary of Thomas Minor, Stonington, Connecticut, 1653–1684* (New London, Conn.: Day Publishing Co., 1899).

Mitchell, Isabel S. *Roads and Road-Making in Colonial Connecticut* (New Haven, Conn.: Yale University Press for Connecticut Tercentenary Commission, 1933).

Mood, Fulmer. "Studies in the History of American Settled Areas and Frontier Lines: Settled Areas and Frontier Lines, 1625–1790" (*Agricultural History*, XXVI (Jan. 1952), 16–34).

Morison, Samuel E. *Builders of the Bay Colony* (Boston: Houghton Mifflin, 1930).

———. *The European Discovery of America: The Northern Voyages* (New York: Oxford University Press, 1971).

———. *The Maritime History of Massachusetts* (Boston: Houghton Mifflin, 1921).

———. *Samuel de Champlain: Father of New France* (Boston: Little, Brown, 1972).

Notestein, Wallace. *The English People on the Eve of Colonization 1603–1630* (New York: Harper and Brothers, 1954).

Original Distribution of the Lands in Hartford Among the Settlers 1639. Vol. XIV of Connecticut Historical Society *Collections* (1912).

Phillips, James D. *Salem in the Eighteenth Century* (Boston: Houghton Mifflin, 1937).

———. *Salem in the Seventeenth Century* (Boston: Houghton Mifflin, 1933).

Pomfret, John E. *Founding the American Colonies 1583–1660* (New York: Harper and Row, 1970).

Powell, Sumner C. *Puritan Village: The Formation of a New England Town.* (Middletown, Conn.: Wesleyan University Press, 1963).

Rowe, William H. *The Maritime History of Maine* (New York: W. W. Norton, 1948).

Rutman, Darrett B. *Husbandmen of Plymouth* (Boston: Beacon Press, 1967).

———. "Governor Winthrop's Garden Crop: The Significance of Agriculture in the Early Commerce of Massachusetts Bay" (*William and Mary Quarterly*, 3rd Series, XX (July 1963), 396–415).

———. "The Pilgrims and Their Harbor" (*William and Mary Quarterly*, 3rd Series, XVII (April 1960), 164–75).

———. *Winthrop's Boston* (Chapel Hill, N.C.: University of North Carolina Press, 1965).

Saltonstall, William G. *Ports of Piscataqua* (Cambridge, Mass.: Harvard University Press, 1941).

Savelle, Max. *The Origins of American Diplomacy* (New York: Macmillan, 1967).

Shurtleff, Harold R. *The Log Cabin Myth* (Cambridge, Mass.: Harvard University Press, 1939).

Shurtleff, Nathaniel B. (ed.). *Records of the Governor and Company of the Massachusetts Bay in New England,* 5 vols. (Boston: William White, 1853–54).

Smith, Page. *As a City Upon a Hill: The Town in American History* (New York: Alfred A. Knopf, 1966).

Sutherland, Stella H. *Population Distribution in Colonial America* (New York: AMS Press, 1966).

Ullman, Edward L. "The Historical Geography of the Eastern Boundary of Rhode Island" (Washington State University *Research Studies,* IV (1939) 67–87).

Van Zandt, Franklin K. *Boundaries of the United States and the Several States.* Geological Survey *Bulletin* 1212 (Washington, D.C.: U.S. Government Printing Office, 1966).

Vaughan, Alden T. *New England Frontier: Puritans and Indians 1620–1675* (Boston: Little, Brown, 1965).

Ward, Harry M. *Unite or Die: Intercolony Relations 1690–1763* (Port Washington, N.Y.: Kennikat Press, 1972).

———. *The United Colonies of New England 1643–1690* (New York: Vantage Press, 1961).

Warden, G. B. *Boston 1689–1776* (Boston: Little, Brown, 1970).

Weeden, W. B. *Early Rhode Island: A Social History of the People* (New York: Grafton Press, 1910).

———. *Economic and Social History of New England 1620–1789.* 2 vols. (Boston: Houghton Mifflin, 1890).

Winthrop, John Jr. "The Description, Culture, and the Use of Maize" (*Philosophical Transactions of the Royal Society of London,* XI-XII (1676–78), No. 142, pp. 1065–69).

Winthrop, John Sr. *Winthrop's Journal: History of New England 1630–1649.* 2 vols. Ed. James K. Hosmer (New York: Barnes & Noble, 1966).

Winthrop Papers. 5 vols. (Boston: Massachusetts Historical Society, 1929–47).

Whitehill, Walter M. *Boston: A Topographical History* (Cambridge, Mass.: Harvard University Press, 1959).

Whitney, Herbert A. "Estimating Precensus Populations: A Method Suggested and Applied to the Towns of Rhode Island and Plymouth Colonies in 1689" (*Annals* of the Association of American Geographers, LV (March 1965), 179–89).

Wright, Louis B. *The Atlantic Frontier* (Ithaca, N.Y.: Cornell University Press, 1959).

Wroth, Lawrence C. *The Voyages of Giovanni da Verrazzano 1524–1528* (New Haven, Conn., Yale University Press, 1970).

Young, Alexander (ed.). *Chronicles of the First Planters of the Colony of Massachusetts Bay* (Boston: Charles C. Little and James Brown, 1846).

Zuckerman, Michael. *Peaceable Kingdom: New England Towns in the Eighteenth Century* (New York: Alfred A. Knopf, 1970).

INDEX

Agriculture: adoption of Indian methods of cultivation, 89; amount of land in cultivation, 93; crops, 91–92; declining production, 72, 99–101; efforts to rejuvenate, 101; experiments with cropping before settlement, 13, 14; fruit trees, 93; initial surplus, 89, 99; kitchen gardens, 93; maize, 30, 89; methods, 99; physical conditions, 90–91, 93, 101; soil depletion, 90; specializations, 99, 102; urban dependence on imports, 51, 100; wheat blast, 92, 101–2

Andover, 72

Animal husbandry: cattle, 95–96; droving, 94, 96; horses, 96, 98–99; need for fences, 94, 97; sheep, 97–98; swine, 97; use of natural forage, 94, 96

Assessments of environment before settlement, 12, 13, 14, 15, 17, 19, 20, 22, 27–29

Bog ores, 126–28, 133

Boston, 39, 73, 75, 80–82, 84, 93, 105, 107, 110, 115, 117

Boundaries: Council for New England, 32–33; Maine and New Hampshire, 34; Massachusetts Bay Colony, 35; Plymouth, 31, 33

Braintree, 55, 127

Cabot, John, 4, 5

Cape Cod, 4, 10, 12, 15, 17, 21, 26, 27, 47, 105, 120

Champlain, Samuel de, 15, 17

Commerce: intraregional, 108, 127, 136, 139; overseas, 73, 75, 83–84, 89, 96, 98, 105, 107–11, 127, 132, 133

Connecticut River, 21, 30, 39, 44, 51

Connecticut Valley, 44, 45, 46, 47, 49, 50, 58

Cosa Mappemonde, 4

Council for New England, 22, 32, 34, 35, 43

Corte Real Brothers, 5

Cultural change, 3, 24, 41, 86

Cuttyhunk (Elizabeth's Isle), 12

Dedham, 72

Dorchester Company, 34, 103

Dutch explorations, 21, 30, 31, 42